Christine's KILIMANJARO

*My Suburban Climb Up
the Mountain of Life*

CHRISTINE M. MALONE

NEW YORK

Christine's KILIMANJARO
My Suburban Climb Up the Mountain of Life

Published in New York, New York, by Morgan James Publishing. Morgan James and The Entrepreneurial Publisher are trademarks of Morgan James, LLC.
www.MorganJamesPublishing.com

The Morgan James Speakers Group can bring authors to your live event. For more information or to book an event visit The Morgan James Speakers Group at www.TheMorganJamesSpeakersGroup.com.

ISBN 978-1-61448-927-6 paperback
ISBN 978-1-61448-928-3 eBook
ISBN 978-1-61448-929-0 audio
ISBN 978-1-61448-930-6 hardcover
Library of Congress Control Number:
2013951455

A free eBook edition is available
with the purchase of this print book.

CLEARLY PRINT YOUR NAME ABOVE IN UPPER CASE

Instructions to claim your free eBook edition:
1. Download the BitLit app for Android or iOS
2. Write your name in **UPPER CASE** on the line
3. Use the BitLit app to submit a photo
4. Download your eBook to any device

Cover Design by:
Rachel Lopez
www.r2cdesign.com

Interior Design by:
Bonnie Bushman
bonnie@caboodlegraphics.com

Photo by:
Simoneau Photography

In an effort to support local communities, raise awareness and funds, Morgan James Publishing donates a percentage of all book sales for the life of each book to Habitat for Humanity Peninsula and Greater Williamsburg.

Get involved today, visit
www.MorganJamesBuilds.com

**Habitat
for Humanity**
Peninsula and
Greater Williamsburg
Building Partner

If you are a lover, come in;
If you are a dreamer, come in;
If you believe that wishes do come true,
Come in and sit with me.
For I have something amazing
To share with you.

Come in…
Come in…

CONTENTS

ACKNOWLEDGMENTS

I wish I had a magic wand. Even just for five minutes. You see I would use this wand to transport myself back into time. To a moment in my youth. To a place in time when I was stuck in utter sadness or pain. To gently take my chin in my hand, look into my own eyes, and say "Breathe, Christine." To believe in moments like this. To tell myself that someday your heart will get an opportunity not only to set their words free, but to thank every wonderful soul that was, is, and will be a part of your life. The magnitude of special people that helped me along the way, to become the woman I am today. Including you. Yes you! The beautiful soul with my book in your hands.

A special thank-you to my guardian angel who is in heaven, Jay Levinson. I feel your pride from the pearly gates above. Thank you for believing in me and all I could be as an author. My heart misses you every day, but I am here with your angel Jeannie, who I equally thank for giving me constant wind under my wings—to keep dreaming, to keep believing. Sharing her love, compassion, and forever friendship with me.

On bended knee I thank everyone for having this chance to share a story through my eyes. To mix my imagination with reality and create the words before you. Most importantly, I thank our Lord for loving his daughter Christine. Unconditionally.

XO Christine

FOREWORD

By JAY CONRAD LEVINSON
"The Father of Guerrilla Marketing"

The first time I met Christine Malone, my wife Jeannie and I were sitting in the waiting room of my oncologist's office. You see, I had recently been diagnosed with myelodysplastic syndrome, a rare form of bone cancer. My marrow had stopped producing red blood cells, and I was dependent on weekly blood transfusions to survive.

Christine was one of Dr. Masri's nurses. Her bright smile and sunny disposition soon became an oasis to us amidst all the tubes and syringes.

After several weeks, she asked me, "So, Jay, what kind of work do you do?" I told her that I was a writer. "Oh, I just love to write!" she said. "I keep a daily journal of my thoughts and experiences; besides nursing, writing is my passion."

I asked her if she would be willing to share with me some of her writings. Timidly, she brought a random stack of her writings the following week for us to take home.

Jeannie and I alternately took turns reading aloud to each other. Some passages would make us roar with laughter, and others would bring us to tears.

Her writing style was a free flow of consciousness akin to that of Dave Eggers in *A Heartbreaking Work of Staggering Genius*, but then again it was really more like a collision of Erma Bombeck meets *Bridget Jones's Diary* meets *Eat, Pray, Love*.

Each week she would bring us another pile of her musings. Eagerly we looked forward to another peek inside her world.

"Christine," I asked her one day, "have you ever considered compiling all these writings into a book?"

"A book?" she questioned sheepishly. "Why, no, I could never write a whole book."

"But you could," I encouraged. "Your writing style is so unique, and you're a wonderful storyteller."

"Do you really think so?" she said, quite astonished

Thus began the exciting journey of seeing the birth of *Christine's Kilimanjaro—My Suburban Climb Up the Mountain of Life* unfold before us, as week after week new layers were peeled back to reveal the heart and soul of this amazing woman.

One of her chapters was especially touching to me. As an oncology nurse, she shared that she had created a "Wall of Remembrance" to honor the patients who had fought the good fight and had finally taken rest.

On the next visit, I asked her to take me to the back of the office where her wall was displayed.

She had painted beautifully framed hearts of different patterns and colors to represent something special about each person. I stood in awe. I felt the thoughtfulness and love that she had poured into each painting.

Gently I squeezed her hand and whispered into her ear, "Be sure to make my heart out of camo."

Editor's Note:
A few months later Jay Conrad Levinson passed peacefully on to his next great adventure...and yes...he has a camo-colored heart mounted proudly on Christine's wall.

A Note to the Reader

Sometimes your dreams can alter your life forever.
That is, if you stop to enjoy the view as you climb.

The heartbeat of *Christine's Kilimanjaro-My Suburban Climb Up the Mountain of Life* started with a promise to God. There I lay, in a puddle of tears one night on my kitchen floor, facing a crossroad in my life. I promised the Lord I would try to let go of my past, love the present, and embrace my future, once and for all.

The very next day, I picked up my pen and started writing a letter to God. As I kept writing out snapshots of my life, this text, *Christine's Kilimanjaro*, became a breathtaking reality right before my eyes. For the first time, I resolved to be my own tour guide up my mountain of life. Finally believing in myself, I was forging a new path instead of plodding along the tired and worn out one I had become accustomed to, discovering something new and no longer impossible along the way.

As I wrote, I learned that life is going to be messy. It is simultaneously hurtful, confusing, amazing, breathtaking, and even magical at times. However, if I don't stop to enjoy my view in the climb, when and if I finally make it to the top, it will be nothing more than that–just the top of a mountain!

So, my journey awaits you. I have one small piece of loving advice to give you, dear reader, before you begin: "Please stay seated! Keep hands and feet inside the moving vehicle at all times! It's going to be a bumpy and wild ride, people!" That is, unless you want to stand up and shout, "WOO-HOO!" with me.

Let's face it. Some rules are meant to be broken!

Love,
Christine

VISION

1

I t was the last Friday in November, officially voted (by me) as my day to chill out! To sit on my couch stuffed full of turkey. To lay like broccoli and veg out in front of the television. That's all I kept telling myself I would do–for now anyways.

Standing with the refrigerator door wide open, I sighed, wishing the hordes of leftovers from Thanksgiving dinner would somehow find their own way to the garbage can. I was thinking to myself, *Really, Christine? Go chill out!*

It was a day of no work, no kids, and no husband—just me and my dogs. My house was clean; no dishes were in the sink, and even the bathrooms were clean. The phone was not ringing to remind me to pay the bills. So why couldn't I relax? Not listening to my own advice, I began wandering around, looking for wet towels. Maybe I would just do one last load of laundry for the day.

The house had a weird echo to it. Yesterday, I had begun my preparation for Christmas by stripping every curio cabinet and every end table of all my regular knickknacks. Now it was as if they were all just waiting around for the Christmas explosion I decorate them in every year.

My goal by the end of today was to make Christmas magic appear, to get a jump on the holiday season that was beginning in less than twenty-four hours. Well, at least in my mind, when December first comes, forget about it. It's the holiday express from there on out.

What a chore that was, listening to my son pull all the boxes down from the attic bright and early that morning. I pleaded with him to please be careful, that many of those boxes were filled with hand-painted ceramic breakables, memories that can never be replaced. I stood and watched helplessly as he tossed the boxes to the floor of my garage, wincing as he told me my stinkin' memories weighed a ton.

I was trying not to feel guilty about the fact that I had not yet purchased one single Christmas gift. Also, my daughter's fifteenth birthday is two days before Christmas, and I had no idea what we were doing for *that* yet. Trust me, that kid's birthday parties are quite the exhausting social event.

Panicking, I quickly wrote the word *cake* in blue crayon on a piece of scrap paper and taped it to the overly cluttered fridge door. I hoped it would be a true reminder: remember your own daughter's birthday cake! To be honest, I knew I would eventually look at the refrigerator and not "see" the paper or word *cake* after a while.

Two years ago, when Em was turning thirteen, we had a big celebration: a holiday party/birthday party. It was a dress-up event, with appetizers and a chocolate fountain, adults in the kitchen, and Top-40 music playing from every speaker. Thinking back, the party was actually quite breathtaking. We had centerpieces filled with fresh flowers, candles floating everywhere, streamers of cloth ribbon, linen tablecloths, and elaborate goody bags for each girl who attended.

About two hours into the party, my husband said to me, "What kind of cake did you get?" I absolutely froze with fear. I had completely forgotten the cake. As I was on the brink of tears, Ed said, "Come on, Christine. It's kind of funny. Relax! Don't worry! I will go get a cake." I didn't say what I was thinking: *It's just two days before Christmas, Ed!* His naivety somehow miraculously made me relax. I did not share with him that you have to special order the cake or it would be decorated in Christmas cheer, not birthday stuff.

He slipped out the door while the girls were ooing and aahing over the gifts. Emily didn't even know he was gone. He did come back with an awesome cookie cake, which was enormous and probably cost him a fortune. She was thrilled and had no clue about the forgotten cake. His smile of achievement said it all. Em hugged him, saying she always wanted a cookie cake the size of Texas.

As the party wound down, Ed and I stood in the empty kitchen, stuffing our faces with overly frosted cookie cake. He reenacted how he had to beg the girl in the bakery to scrape off the giant menorah in the middle of the cookie and pleaded with the entire bakery staff to just put Emily's name on it. He even offered cash on the side, holding up a twenty-dollar bill for anyone who could make this happen. My sugar buzz was making me laugh wildly at his Tony Soprano impersonation and negotiation skills. I have to be honest; it impressed me quite a bit.

Back from my reverie, I found myself leaning against the wall, looking at the fifteen or so Christmas boxes. I was uninterested in any of it. The thought of decorating right now was exhausting, probably because I had enough holiday cheer to decorate two houses.

All I had been really wishing for lately was an hour of quiet, and here I was with plenty of it—still not allowing myself to relax! I began looking around the family room for the remote. I wanted to turn on the television and distract my mind from another to-do list.

While digging my hands into the couch cushions, I was shouting out to my little Chihuahua, "*Carpe Diem*, Katie!" My words got her all excited, thinking I was saying the words, "Cheese, Katie!" Finding the remote was more challenging than I expected.

I was thinking to myself, *Seize the day, Christine. Don't you dare give up on that remote! You deserve a few television programs; you pay a fortune in satellite TV!* I finally found the remote, held it up to the ceiling, and said, "You will keep me still for more than five minutes! Do you hear me, remote?" laughing as I spoke. Not only did I look ridiculous, but I had also perplexed my dog. She left the room with a "whatever" waddle and went back to her crate to take a late-morning nap.

Flipping through the one thousand or so channels with my now sacred remote, I felt like a mad scientist, hoping to find anything other than reality TV. Finally I gave in and stopped at the *Real Housewives* television show.

I thought, *Really? Come knock on my door, Bravo. I will show you reality!* I was mumbling under my breath, "I would never, ever, not in a million years, pay four grand for high heels with red soles!" But then I shouted out loud, like I had company, "Never say never, Christine!"

I was flipping frantically through the morning lineup when I found the OWN channel. *Hey! I forgot Oprah had her own network!* I always got frustrated when she announced her new network was "coming soon," but now it was here. I always thought OWN should be an acronym for "Outstanding Women Now" or something catchy, something with spice. But, if I had hordes of money like Oprah, I suppose I would name everything after myself too. "Do you like my new CMM?" I would say, as I showed my friends my new recliner? Hysterical!

All of a sudden I became completely transfixed with the TV. (This is not rare for me.) An old episode of *Oprah* had sparked my interest. Her new network was playing a marathon of her old show, and I judged, by how her hair was styled, that this episode was probably from 2000-ish.

Oprah was standing at the edge of her stage, holding her microphone up to her chin with both of her hands. Two teenage girls were talking to her from the audience. They were speaking to Oprah with such happiness that I found myself scooting to the edge of the couch. Each girl took turns talking about her hopes, wishes, dreams, and future plans.

When one of the girls finished, she smiled at Oprah and pulled out a giant piece of poster board. This board was laced with words: catchy words, inspirational phrases, where she wanted to go to college, a picture of a wedding dress. Then she stopped speaking and pointed to the bottom corner of her board. The camera zoomed in to show the viewers at home. Written in pink marker in the corner of her board, it said, "Be on the *Oprah* show." *Okay! Now I am interested,* I think to myself.

The greatest part about this whole episode was discovering that these two girls had accomplished every single thing on the poster board–except being on *Oprah*. Now, this young girl was standing in the audience, showing the world her "vision board," and making her last vision come true! The girls went on to explain that their vision boards were a tool they used, a magical tool that they had designed to awaken their subconscious. They went on to say that we at home could create our own vision boards! We could put our dreams, our hopes, and our wishes on a poster—no matter how crazy our thoughts might sound! It would motivate us and help our dreams bubble to the surface! Creating a board could help make possible what you once thought was impossible!

All I could think was, *I cannot wait for Emily to get home from school!* Looking at the clock, I saw it would be thirty minutes exactly until we could zoom down the street and get our supplies.

I paced like a caged animal, waiting for her bus to appear at the end of the driveway. Moving into the kitchen, I found myself chanting, "Vision, vision!"

"Mom, are you home?" Emily shouted out like we live in a castle, not a 1,600 square foot home.

"Hey there, Em. Quick, go to the bathroom. I have something very exciting planned for us!" Running up to her, I patted her backside in hopes she would speed it up.

"Mom, unless you didn't put the Christmas stuff up yet because we are going to Disney, I am not interested. I am so tired! My teachers were so cranky today. I want to just go and chill out." She didn't even wait for my response. Following her through the house to her bedroom, I watched her fall onto her bed like a freshly chopped oak tree.

Taking her a cold soda as a hopeful bribe, I sat at the foot of her bed and started telling her about the episode of *Oprah* I just watched. I explained that we were going to make our own vision boards to motivate and inspire our subconscious. Didn't that sound fun?

Unfortunately, the last part came out more like a question. The bloodhound in her was all over it as she can sniff out my weaknesses better than anyone on this earth.

"You tell me, Mom. You don't sound so sure. Is this something we need to do, like, this very minute?" she asked me while turning on a fully charged iPhone and rolling over on her side to face the wall. I knew that once her device got to surfing and Instagram-ing, I was as good as done–no creative mother/daughter art projects would take place tonight.

"How about this? I will go and get all the supplies, while you stay here, hang out, and rest. You can listen to music. But, when I get back, you have to promise we will do this." I stood perfectly still with my hands folded like I was begging her. She glanced over her shoulder and winced at my theatrical plea.

"What about the tree? You said we would put the tree up tonight. Come on, Mom. You know how you flip out if the tree is still in the box the first week of December!" Now she had her hand on her hip, but she was still facing the wall. I began biting at my bottom lip because her truth serum has a stinging taste to it.

"I promise. Promise! We will put the tree up tomorrow night. We'll start a new tradition. Every November 30th, the tree goes up. Plus, Dad will be home tomorrow morning. Let's wait until he is home. What do you say?" I crossed my fingers like a schoolgirl behind my back, praying she would come with me.

All I heard was annoyed huffing sounds, but then she shot me a thumbs up, and said, "Yeah, okay, Mom. I guess."

Standing behind her, I started clapping my hands as if I had won an all-expenses-paid vacation to Italy.

"Okay! I will be back in one hour. Does that sound good? Are you sure you don't want to go for a ride?" I hoped that if I asked one more time, she would come with me.

"Nope. I am still staying!" was all I could get out of her.

I found myself looking through hundreds of used magazines at the thrift store. I wasn't sure exactly what I wanted. But, for a quarter a piece, they were all coming home with me. That night, Emily and I spent hours cutting out sayings, inspirational words, beautiful pictures, and poems. Then we strategically placed all these cut-out items in different spots on giant pieces of poster board, showing each other before we made it permanent by gluing them down.

My vision board is hanging on my wall above my computer desk in my bedroom. I look at it every day, sometimes three or four times a day. Now that I sit and *really* look at it, it makes me smile.

I know deep down my book, this book, is my biggest and best dream. *Christine's Kilimanjaro* is my bright and shiny mountain that I have never given up on climbing. It speaks to me. My Kilimanjaro breathes the tribal hum of the African drums into my dreams, helping me to believe in the author I have always wanted to be.

Some nights when I cannot sleep, I think about the real, tiny wooden box that sits at the highest summit of this majestic mountain, Kilimanjaro. This box holds a journal, and every person who makes it to the top records his experiences and accomplishments in this magical journal. It sits waiting for the person who finds it to record her victory story. My heart sings and skips a beat just thinking about the moving messages left in this journal!

So, here I sit, writing down snapshots of my life and making it happen! Hmmm, making what happen? I guess I want to make the story of my life happen in print, with added doses of my imagination.

I dream of being on the best-seller list, making people laugh, cry, and hopefully want more. Maybe I will even inspire someone else to write her own story. Maybe someone will say, "Damn! That girl can write!" Maybe someone will say, "What complete junk!" and sell it at her next garage sale for a quarter. I don't know.

But, to have my story bound neatly in a book?
To have my Kilimanjaro journal in my hands—dare I dream?
Good Lord.
Pure Heaven!
But, for now, it's my vision, and only time will tell.

My Vision Board

Remember: with God ALL things are possible!

Tell someone everyday, "Hey, you're awesome!"

Spend a whole day of dancing with One Direction and Emily.

Learn how to say NO without apologizing and laugh without worrying!

Meet Oprah and have lunch. Laugh out loud with Tom Hanks. Have Adam Sandler over for dinner.

Hug Ellen and high five Julia Roberts.

Share a piece of birthday cake with Will Ferrell.

Be in a bike marathon and finish!

Have a fabulous Christmas in NYC (White Christmas).

Learn how to really play the piano ("Imagine" by John Lennon). THEN, sing it to Bono!

Travel to Italy and learn Italian.

Success occurs when opportunity meets preparation. (Oh, YES it does!)

Four star family vacation at Walt Disney World.

Drink more water; feel confident in a bathing suit (finally).

No more fat "mom" jeans. Come on! You can do the skinny jeans again. Come on, girl!

Be financially free, with no more money drain.

Visit with my mom and sister; have a girls' night out with our daughters.

Fly to Ohio and visit Grandma Rose, Grandma Billie, and Papa's graves.

You have the power to change a child's life in Africa!

My story needs to be a movie-making blockbuster. Write it down. Make it happen, Christine!

Christine? Make it a great day or not–the choice is yours!

Be the star you were destined to be. Write your story with flare!

Today is the day I write my own story and become the author I dreamed of!

Let your children know (every day) that they WILL change the world for the better!

Believe in positive thinking, rainbows, and love. And never give up!

Meet someone in 2013 who changes your life/career forever, for
the better!

Just know, if you don't think you're awesome, don't get mad if others
don't think you are either!

Be the change you want to see in the world.

If you don't know what to say, just smile!

Do you, Christine, have passion?

Love is all you need.

One simple word: believe!

A BOOK? 2

It's actually quite hysterical, the reactions people have had when I told them I was writing a book after creating my vision board. I've got to be honest: I was feeling more comfortable by the day talking about my book. Well, kind of.

One Friday, my coworker asked me the dreaded question, the question I hate more than anything on a Friday afternoon: "What are you doing this weekend?"

I responded as quickly as I could, then immediately threw one of my fingers in my mouth and began to chew on an already very sore cuticle. Note: this is something you never want to do in healthcare–no matter how nervous you are!

"Writing my book, you know, my autobiography," I said to her quickly as I held my breath, peeking out of one eye at her.

"What? What on earth about?" She didn't miss a beat, and the insane cuticle biting didn't distract her. She responded with a look on her face like I was speaking in foreign tongues.

"Oh, about my life, me, I guess," I said to her in a sing-song tone, hoping and praying that would be enough, hoping she would drop the subject.

Just when I thought I could grab my purse from the bottom drawer of my desk and get out of there, a couple of my coworkers rounded the corner and asked, "What's all the talking about?"

"She's writing a book, she guesses. I would never have the time to just sit and write. Christine thinks she is the next JK Rowling," my coworker said, flicking her pen in my direction, but never looking my way for even a second.

In my mind, I tried to dismiss her unkind comment. I thought, *Wow, JK Rowling! That is an enormous compliment! However, I am not British; I am not a single mother. Hello? My book is not about wizards and stuff. I just told you it's about me, but maybe my sequel should be about an ordinary girl who finds a wand buried in her back yard and uses it to erase passive-aggressive people like you! Whoosh, bye, bye!*

One of the two curious coworkers started cackling away about every book she had read since first grade, and I began to drift to that comfortable place in my mind. I thought, *Maybe I should keep this project as my own little secret for now.*

A smile covered my face as I thought, *One day, BAM! I am on the TODAY Show. No, sorry, ladies, I can't come in tomorrow; I'm taking the red-eye flight to New York. Yep, going to be on TODAY—just me and my book!*

As my thoughts drifted back to the stale, overly clean office, I heard this sweet, almost child-like, monotone voice. Lord, she has moved from titles to authors: Dan Brown, Judy Blume, Sidney Sheldon, Judith McNaught, Steven King, on and on. I don't even think she knew she was talking anymore.

She reminded me of Bubba from *Forrest Gump,* naming his favorite kinds of shrimp: lemon shrimp, fried shrimp, creole shrimp, popcorn shrimp, teriyaki shrimp…Hysterical, I started giggling as I stared at her jabbering away.

My other coworker still sat quietly, thinking carefully about her response. The blink, blink of her eyes was all I got out of her. However, I could tell she was thinking.

The other just blurted out after she was done naming hundreds of random authors, "Oooooh, is it a book about recipes and crafts?"

I gave her a much-longer-than-normal pause. My delayed response would have made most people blurt out, "Hello, answer me!" But there she sat; she even pulled her chair closer to me. She waited for my response with this over-the-rainbow, Looney Tunes smile. Clasping her hands tightly together, she leaned forward, waiting and wanting to explode in applause. I thought carefully. For once I decided to think before I spoke.

My throat was so dry; I don't even think my response was audible. Is this what disappointing people with my book would feel like? I said softly, "Crafts, and recipes? Whaaaat?"

She nodded like a two-year-old when asked if he wants ice cream before dinner.

I so wanted to tell her, "Yes! It's about the long-lost art of how to hand sew throw pillows and how to make the perfect fondue!" Instead, I let out a sentence in one breath, not daring to pause: "No, it's about me, my memory of my life, the past, the present, and the future."

"Oh, poo. I was hoping to give you some ideas for a chapter or two! Wouldn't that have been neat?" she said as she twirled in her chair thinking about it.

All I could come up with was, "Yeah, neat-o." *What the heck?* I don't think I have ever said *neat-o* since I was seven or eight! Now, all I could think in my mind was, *I have got to go home! This book is exhausting. Why did I even start telling people?*

I tried to push her swivel chair and her very happy, crafty self to the right of my desk so that I could grab my purse and make a run for it. Looking over at her smiling at me, I decided I couldn't leave her hanging. So, I said to her gently, "You know, you should write a book about crafts and recipes. You would be good at that!"

She smiled brightly, wheeled her chair over to another area of the room, and began frantically texting to someone. Then I heard her say, "Great! We should all write a book. We should be a medical office full of writers. That would be neat-o." Then she laughed and snorted in a tone that said, "I am so annoyed with you."

The third coworker, who was once silent, quickly piped up and said, "Well, if it's about you and your life, are we in your book?"

Immediately they all became quiet, like pin-drop quiet. Although Ms. Crafty was thrilled at the prospect of doing a chapter together, her face revealed what she thought about being mentioned in my book.

"No, no, don't worry. It is a book about me, my crazy stories, and stuff like that." I started thinking to myself that maybe my response sounded a little weird (About me?), but they seemed okay with it.

As I rode the elevator down with them to the first floor, their silence was unbearable. Tilting my head to the speaker above me, I tried to focus on the music. But that just made me feel worse than their uncomfortable silence.

My stomach felt as though someone was squeezing it from the inside out. The tune playing was U2 in elevator music form. Bono? I started flashing back to parking my junior year to this exact song with a boy I thought was a boyfriend, the guy my father only referred to as "needle dick." *What's next?* I thought, *Am I going to get shocked from the time clock when I punch out?*

Descending three floors was taking an eternity. *What in the world? I am going to call facilities Monday to see if they realize and elevator is…*The doors suddenly opened with an ear-popping "ding!"

My happy dolphin of a friend and coworker stopped and turned to me. (I call her happy dolphin because she reminds me of those dolphins you can swim with for the day. Her happiness is always all in, all over, from head to toe.) She gives me a bear hug. She is five feet tall, while I am six feet tall. Her hugs always make me feel better, no matter what my mood is. She says to me, while squeezing me tightly, "I am proud of you!" She is still smiling from head to toe as we turn to wave good-bye. All I could think was, *I work in oncology; one out of three is not bad at all.* I reassure myself, *Relax already, Christine, those are good odds.*

Still smiling from her happy squeeze of a hug as I drove home with no radio on, I tried to allow my brain to readjust. I was thinking, *Pull it together. Who said writing a book was easy?* I started laughing at the very words *easy* and *book* in the same sentence, knowing this book might be the most challenging thing I have done yet–well, besides trying on my skinny jeans after I eat pizza.

Dragging my overly tired body in the front door, I felt happy knowing that I would get to sleep past 5:15 tomorrow. I was frozen in shock, however, when I saw the house. It looked like a bomb had gone off! Backpacks were lying on the threshold, shoes were everywhere, and big, sweaty cups filled with red fruit punch sat teetering on the carpet. Plus, a giant puddle of dog pee sat exactly where I take my shoes off every day. It was as if my little dog was telling me, "Hello, you're late!" I realized this was way too much mess for my two kids. I decided that they must have friends over and was thankful that I hadn't started screaming for them to come to me, front and center!

I headed straight for my room to take off my scrubs. Putting on my robe, I lay in silence on my bed. I was contemplating whether I had enough energy to bring my teens out of their electronic caves to come and help me pick up this pigsty of a house.

Just then, I heard my phone ring, and it was my friend from the hospital. I used to work at the hospital before I transferred to the doctor's office. I shiver even thinking about working at the hospital as I had to work three twelve-hour shifts in a row. How on earth did I survive that for a year?

When I answered, I heard her sweet and lovable voice saying, "Hey, girl, is that you? Do you want to go out tonight?" Like it hadn't been nine months since we had seen each other, maybe five months since we had texted a single word to one another. But, that's what I love about her. No excuses.

"No, I can't tonight. I am staying in to write," I replied, like I party all the time but just couldn't make it this one time. Hell, if my pajamas are not on by eight o'clock at night, you'd think the world was coming to an end for me! Complete silence from her.

So I said again, in a matter-of-fact tone, "A book, you know, my autobiography."

"Christine, are you having a nervous breakdown? Maybe I should take you to get something tattooed? Yeah, we're going to go get ourselves some Skinny Girl Sangria and then go get tats!"

Not in a million years would I ever associate writing a book with a nervous breakdown–like, ever! I just started laughing until I almost couldn't breathe! This response only made her more convinced that I was having a nervous breakdown. Maybe she thought the word *autobiography* meant breakdown? This was a first!

"Yep, my cousin Nancy had a nervous breakdown when she was fifty, too!"

She started rambling about Nancy's kids and her broke-ass husband. She talked, and I tried to bring her words into my brain. I began to realize that she was serious! And, wait a minute! Reverse. I am only forty-three! Did she just say fifty?

"Hey, wait! Helloooo, no nervous breakdown, no sangria, no tats. Lord, that is the last thing I need right now!" I blurted out to her as she kept talking about her cousin Nancy's breakdown.

I was hoping she would get the point. The last thing I need, when I walk over to the hospital cafeteria to buy a disgustingly overpriced muffin, is for people to give me the look that says, *Ohh, poor Christine, we heard you had a breakdown. Hug!*

Lord, how did I get twisted into this mess? *Note to self: STOP telling random people about your book!*

She didn't really care, though. I could have told her I peed my pants while standing in the grocery store checkout line. She had another call and said in one full breath, "Okay. Good luck with that! If you change your mind, we are all going to Cowboys tonight!" and hung up.

I just lay my very heavy head slowly to my pillow and let my eyes close. Still trying to process my day, I heard the beating drums of Africa rolling around in my mind.

My day: woke up at five thirty; overpampered my teenage daughter; walked two dogs; took out the garbage to the curb–all while my teenage son slept peacefully; did a quick load of towels; washed dishes, because the dishwasher is still broken; went to work an eight-hour day taking care of cancer patients; paid bills on my break; ate a disgusting, smashed PB&J for lunch; spoke out loud about my book; and was accused of a nervous breakdown while being invited out for sangria and tattoos.

Truth is, I look forward to opening my journal and pouring out my heart each night. Actually, come four o'clock, no matter where I am at the moment, my mind drifts to all the words I have stacked and crammed into my mind. I sit at my computer and write this book because bringing my story to life is my dream. It's almost like the blinds of my mind are drawn, not allowing anything else in, until I set my words free.

A Girl Can Dream 3

Moving into the kitchen, I saw my daughter sitting at the table. I can't hide my enormous grin. It's a Friday night, and she is sitting at the table with homework that is not due until Monday. Just looking at my organized daughter makes me feel proud she did not inherit my it-is-Sunday-night-and-I-have-two-papers-due-tomorrow type of mind.

"Emily, do you want beef or chicken tacos?" She gave me a shrug of her shoulders, then looked over and smiled at me. I am guessing that my robe at six o'clock pm with a pony tail and goggle glasses was pretty hysterical to her.

"How was your day, Em? Was it a peach or a pit?" I asked her as I plopped ground beef into a skillet.

Since the kids were little, we have always done the peach and pit question after school or at the dinner table. I started this tradition because whenever I would ask them about their day, all I ever got was "fine"–no matter how many different ways I asked. Always the same answer, "Fine." Plus, the peach analogy is from one of our favorite stories, *James and the Giant Peach*.

So, the peach is something good. The pit is something, well, horrible. This way, they get to pick and choose what they share. Occasionally, my daughter texts me at work, "Peach: A+ on Spanish test"; it makes me smile.

"Let me think about that for a minute. Most of my day was a pit, but for you, Mom, I will find a peach!" She was grinning with her answer, looking intently at her phone and surfing *whatever* frantically with her thumb.

Instead of waiting, I decided to start my fantasy out loud. Emily and I love to talk about our plans when my book becomes a best seller. At first she thought the idea was crazy. She hates "what ifs," or so she is always telling me. "I am a realist, Mom!" But, I knew, as I painted some verbal scenarios for her, I would eventually spark her interest.

She is an excellent listener. Truly, it is a gift of hers. It actually amazes me, how comfortable she is with listening. I, on the other hand, have a hard time with this skill. I drift in and out, and I stare at people's teeth, wondering how long that black piece of whatever has been wedged in their teeth. Yes, it is called ADD. But, I have lived this long without being officially diagnosed. Why start now?

"So, Em, I was thinking that when Ellen calls us, you know, to ask us to come on her show, I bet she will she will say something like, 'Hey! Hello, there! This is Ellen. I was wondering if this is the woman who wrote that funny book? Let me just tell you, I love the book! So, I need you to come on out, chat on my show, and tell me all about this climb of your life. You know, you can even bring your awesome daughter, and you could both be on my show!'" I paused my imagination for a moment to look over at Emily. I saw her peek over her iPhone and tilt her head in my direction. Her energy said she was listening. So I kept talking to see how far I could go with this.

"I will tell her, 'You are so awesome, Ellen. Thank you! But, I have a question, or a favor, to ask. My daughter would love to meet One Direction–especially Harry!' Ellen will start laughing and say, 'Hey, I know those boys. I will give them a call! So, come on out. Get out here and bring your daughter! Just don't forget that fabulous book of yours!'" I ended my verbal fantasy and tried not to giggle. I bit my lip, thinking to myself, *Wow! I am kind of proud of my stellar, on-the-spot imagination!*

Hook, line, and sinker! I got her now! My daughter's fascination for British boys–especially one with the name of Harry–is my secret weapon to get her to talk to me. If she shuts down, I simply ask, "So, what's Harry been up to?"

"Would you really say that?" she asked, without a trace of facial expression whatsoever.

So, I think to myself, *Enjoy this! Go crazy!* But here's the deal. It's not crazy; it's all on my vision board. She just doesn't realize it yet.

"Yes, of course! I would be okay with asking Ellen to help us spend a whole day dancing with One Direction! Then, I would say to her, 'Ellen, strike a pose. Go on, girl!' Then WE dance!"

Smirking to myself, with my back to the kitchen table where she sat, I wished I could tell her how I sounded like Sprockets from SNL! Her long, huffing sigh made me realize I was on thin ice. If I even attempt to start dancing like Sprockets, she would lock herself in her room until morning. So I moved forward with a question I know will be okay: "What would you wear if we got to go on *Ellen*?" Talking about clothes with Emily is an easy transition. I pray.

"If I were to play your silly game, and if, by some miracle, we got to be on *The Ellen Show* and One Direction was there," she paused and asked, "Will there be any other guests?"

I know she is having fun–even though her device hasn't left her grip. She was looking at me, waiting to see what was next.

"Oh, yeah, of course there will be! Ellen will pull out all the stops. Tom Hanks will be there. He will laugh until his sides hurt from watching all of us dancing! Then, Adam Sandler will call in and ask if he can come to our house for spaghetti and meatballs. All of the sudden, Will Ferrell will come walking around the corner, interrupting the phone call. He is already eating a huge bowl of spaghetti and wearing a sauce-stained bib. Will will stop and shout to Adam on the phone, 'Sorry! Too late, pal. I've already been there!' Then. as he shovels in a mouthful, he will ask Ellen if she wants a bite!"

Emily knows these are some of my favorite actors. I will watch anything with them in it. Heck, to get my son to laugh off a bad mood, I quote Ricky Bobby. This is one of my favorite Will Ferrell characters. Okay, it is probably not one of my gold-star parenting moments, but it always makes my son laugh off not winning a baseball game. I start by talking in the character's hillbilly accent, and then I do the trademark line from the movie: "If you aint' first, you're last!" That last sentence must be read in your best redneck twang. The top of this list of actors, for me, is, of course, Chris Farley and John Candy. I let out a long sigh, thinking about missing them. Shaking off my sadness, I looked over at Emily.

I actually saw the smallest smile start to form on her face. She started laughing, a sound I never tire of hearing. Wow, I tried to recall the last time I heard this laugh.

"Okay, just don't, like, scare Tom Hanks with the crazy bug eyes you make when you get excited. And, don't freak out Ellen with your insane laugh." She started hiccupping from laughing, and this made us both start laughing.

"I think they would all like you, though, Mom. And, I would straighten my hair and wear a One Direction t-shirt, my favorite jeans, and my pink Converse. Ellen loves shoes, you know." She then went back to typing the Instagram thingy, or was it her twitter?

"Would you dance with Ellen? If I promised not to dance, would you dance?" I asked her as I bounced in place at the stove, finishing up my taco fiesta.

She squished up her face, "Really, Mom? You know as well as I do that you would not miss an opportunity to dance with Ellen! You would probably push a grandma down to be able to dance with Ellen!" She found her analogy a little too funny and began snickering behind the small phone screen. But, for the moment, our space felt happy.

Taking my chance, I started really dancing around. I pretended to shout out to Ellen, "Ellen, please tell Emily I have some serious moves!" I began laughing breathlessly as I performed in my kitchen, acting as if I were back at Studio 54. I encouraged Emily to throw down, to just get up and dance too! I instantly began twirling her as soon as she stood up, for fear she would run to her room. Her ringing phone sounded off with an incoming text. This quickly ended our dance-a-thon with a cheerful high five. I was thinking to myself as I gathered our plates for dinner, *When was the last time I just let loose like that? Maybe that fun girl isn't too far buried after all.*

We fixed our tacos at the stove, then found our seats at the little kitchen table that has been in the same spot for fifteen years. We talked about her day: Spanish, it's hard; computer is beyond boring; math is ridiculous, because there are forty-five kids in her class and the teacher is always calling her by the wrong name.

However, she was watching *The Wizard of Oz* in her film class, so she told me about oddities in the film not everyone notices–unless you are like her weird film teacher who has seen *The Wizard of Oz* a trillion times.

Out of the clear blue sky, she looked up with a serious expression. I stopped chewing, not understanding what her dramatic pause was about.

"Mom, I want to be the one to tell you something, okay? I don't think Oprah is going to find her way to your book, or like, just call you on the phone. She only sent you a generic letter last time; she probably sent the exact same letter to thousands of people."

I found myself not being able to swallow my taco, so I spit it into my napkin for fear I would get taco lodged in my windpipe.

"Yeah, I know, Em. But, it's okay to dream once in a while, right?" She shrugged her shoulders as she masterfully plopped more sour cream on her plate and responded to a text at the same time.

She is referring to the letter I sent to *The Oprah Winfrey Show* about two years ago.

I had been in a horrifying car accident. It was Tuesday, a normal day. I had just dropped Em off at school and swung by the dollar store. I was sitting at a red light right by our library, less than a mile from my home, when I was hit by a drunk driver at nine o'clock in the morning. He never took his foot off the gas. He was traveling 52 mph, and I was his brick wall.

The whole tragic scene is something my memory can pull up like it was thirty minutes ago. Sometimes, I still have nightmares where I am hit over and over again. It's exhausting.

I was waiting behind one car at the red light when I decided to reach across the passenger seat to grab an ABBA CD off the floor. It was actually crammed way up in the far corner, and I was really reaching for it. I was actually lying across the passenger seat when I was hit. I did not see a thing.

After much reflection, all I can really remember is hearing explosions of crushing steal. I can remember the back of my van felt suspended off the ground. I could feel a sensation of spinning and turning as I braced myself against the console of the dash, but the momentum would not allow me to sit up. I could hear explosions of glass all around me, but I did not understand how I should shield my own body. The car was filling with thick smoke, and the burning rubber smell was making me gasp. I could feel–and hear–my van pushing hard against the car in front of me. When I peeked over the dash, I could see that the front of my van had demolished the back end of the car in front of me. We were edging closer to oncoming traffic. I know I was screaming. I think I was screaming, "Please, God…" Somehow, I walked out of this horrific scene unscathed.

I remember sitting up thinking, *What the heck?* It really was like that freeze-frame moment you watch in movies. You know, where everything is happening in slow motion? Like when you see the hero in the movie walking through an explosive battlefield, but all you can hear is his breathing and his heart beating? That is freeze frame!

Then, all of the sudden, I heard pounding and shouting. It was a gurgling sound, almost as if I was under water. I looked out my window, only to see a man I did not recognize. He was screaming through the glass, "Are you okay?"

I can remember just saying, "What?" over and over. I could hear myself saying, "What? What?" as I held my head in my hands, consumed with complete confusion.

The stranger pried the door open, reached in my van, and grabbed my hands. He helped me safely walk to the curb. He said something to me, which I didn't understand, before he ran back to the accident to help others.

Within the blink of an eye, he was gone. I stood alone in the hot Florida sun, not moving a muscle. There was a quiet inside me that I had never felt before. Even as the chaos unfolded before me, everything inside was quiet.

I can remember holding my arms out in front of me, to see if there was blood. I touched my face and pulled my hand back to check there, too. No blood. I remember leaning to my right to look through the smashed window on the passenger side of my van. I was checking to see if I was dead and my body was still in the van. No one was coming near me, so I thought, *I must be dead.*

Everyone was moving around me, not paying me any attention. In fact, police officers and firemen were all shouting with their hands cupped over their mouths, "Has anyone, ANYONE seen the driver of this van?" While pointing to the wreckage I just walked away from, they all ran around asking other accident victims, "Where is this driver?" I just stood there, not speaking a word. For a moment, I wasn't sure they could even see me, but they were looking right at me.

When I finally had the courage to raise my hand towards the rescue worker just inches from my body, I said quietly, "I am the driver of this van." He just waved his hand at me like, "Uh-oh, crazy accident gawkier," and turned and walked away. So, I just kept standing there completely silent. I frantically began scanning my eyes through the massive crowd of people. I was hoping to see the guy with the red beard and white shirt who had pulled me out. My angel?

Firemen brought in huge hoses to clean all the spilled fuel off the road. Police and emergency workers were assisting people involved in the crash into ambulances. Some police were moving traffic, while some were waving the tow truck drivers in to clear the road of wrecked cars.

All of the sudden, I heard, "Chris! Chris?" My husband's best friend of thirty years just happened to be in Orange City that day to look at a boat motor. He was eight cars back when it happened. He had gotten out of his truck to walk up through the cars to see what the commotion was about when he saw me standing there.

A tow truck driver pulled up to scene of the accident to remove the twisted metal that was once my van. He hopped out of his cab and walked up to me. He leaned in and said, "Lady, can I hug you? I thought you were as good as dead when that car hit you. I followed that guy for five miles on the phone with 911. He was all over the road. I was praying for you, for the person he hit!" It was still not really registering in my head what he was saying to me. He just hugged me like a rag doll and started reciting the Lord's Prayer in my ear.

Up on the sidewalk, away from the scene, the guy who hit me was walking a white chalk line. Well, I am not sure you want to call it walking. He could barley stand. Next to him and his chalk line, the police were laying out drugs and booze bottles from his car. My husband's friend overheard him say to the police, "I was texting my friend. What happened?" He was taken to an ambulance in handcuffs.

Finally, when the emergency workers realized I was the driver of the van, they could not believe their eyes. They assisted me to a sitting position on the curb and took my blood pressure. They whispered amongst themselves as they pointed to my destroyed van, "She was the driver of that van!" After much deliberation in a secretive group huddle, they agreed my husband's friend could take me home, and I did not have to go to the hospital.

I could not sleep for days. I also became obsessed with the guy who saved me. I called everyone I knew to see if they knew this person, describing his appearance over and over to everyone I talked to. I never had any luck. I think I was worried I was the only one who had seen this man.

Yes, I believe in angels. Obviously, mine were working overtime that day. But, I am a girl who wants the answers. However, no one had a clue as to who or what I was talking about. Even my husband's friend didn't have a clue.

So, what did I do? After a couple of days of thinking, I sat down and wrote the CEO of the hospital I worked at. I asked him in a matter-of-fact email if we could start a pledge, a no-texting-while-driving pledge. I explained that we had an incredible opportunity to save lives. He emailed me back in less than five minutes, asking me to come to his office first thing the next morning.

I spent months planning and organizing with the hospital's marketing team to pull this off. Posters lined the walls on the way to the cafeteria, all featuring the CEO and me: *Do Not Text and Drive!*

The hospital even had blue rubber bracelets made that said, "Don't Text and Drive!" We decided whomever signed the pledge would get a bracelet. Actually, everyone in the hospital received one.

I then sent my amazing story to Oprah at *The Oprah Winfrey Show* to let her know she had inspired me to, as Gandhi said, "Be the change I wish to see in the world." While we did not adopt her texting pledge, we were moving mountains just the same.

The day had finally arrived to kick off the whole campaign. Before going to the hospital, I decided to take my daughter to breakfast for a celebration. Sitting at a table in the back, I looked up and in walked the man with the red beard, the guy wearing the white shirt from my accident. I rubbed my eyes to make sure he was real. He did not see me, but I watched him very curiously for about ten minutes. I wanted to soak in this man and his heroic acts. Plus, I asked my daughter about five times, "You see him, right? "

One of the officers at the scene of the accident that day told me that if this man didn't pull me out, I might have died from carbon dioxide poisoning. My van never shut off, and when the muffler came loose with the force of the crash, it pushed a pipe into my hatch.

This was another slow motion moment for me, one of my many movie-freeze-frame moments in my life that I can remember so clearly. I can still feel every step I took and hear my heart thumping. For weeks I had asked the Lord please to let me thank this man. Please, Lord, just let me meet this man. Now, here was my moment. What would I say? I walked up to his table with my head down. He recognized me immediately and smiled a wide grin. He simply stood and hugged me. He hugged me so tightly. I don't think I have ever felt such love for a stranger.

We both stood there smiling and not saying a word. I began to tear up. I looked up to him and blurted out, "Thank you." He smiled and said, "No, thank you." He got teary eyed himself. I stood there looking at him with a very puzzled expression. He told me that he had changed lanes seconds before the accident. He would have been the car that was hit, but he changed lanes. He could not sleep since the accident. For months, he had worried about what happened to me. Seeing me standing here before him was his prayer answered.

"Synchronicity," was all I could say as I smiled warmly. He leaned in and hugged me even more tightly and said, "Or serendipity."

That is a brief synopsis of the letter I wrote and sent to Oprah. However, the generic letter I received in response was "Oprah" talking about the hiatus she was on after ending her talk show. I was actually on a letter loop, getting generic daily updates of her journey to explore what the next life chapter would hold for her. The letters were about beautiful little inspirational things, simple things, like eating pizza with truffles, sitting on her porch reading, or enjoying things like gardening.

It made Emily so frustrated when I would yell from my computer desk, "Letter from Oprah, Em." She would come and listen, hoping and praying this was my special letter.

So, I understand her being bitter. However, miraculously she starts her own little scenario. I believe in my heart that she saw the pain on my face that naturally appears when I think of that accident and my disappointment with the Oprah letter.

"Well, Mom, what about Julia?" she asks me as she pushes away her plate and reaches for her math book to start counting up the problems that were assigned.

Now, this is *my* hook, line, and sinker. She knows Julia Roberts is my all time fav. You see, when I think of Julia, I always say, "Julia Change-the-World Roberts."

I know that's a very big, pretentious title to live up to. But, it's true, and I love her. Her portrayal of Erin Brockovich was spellbinding. A piece of me loves that movie because she is an ordinary girl like me, trying to make a difference in this world. Plus, come on, who could ever forget this line from *Notting Hill*: "I am just a girl, standing in front of a boy, asking him to love her"? Hello! My heart about exploded with that line!

"Well, I think we need Julia's star power to help us with the children in Africa, Em." I see her thinking about Africa and her math that is too difficult for me now. She continues calculating the problems in her math book, but I see her give me a sideways glance.

"Do you know the magic we could do with her help? We could finally open a house for the children of Africa with special needs. You know, Emily, they need us as much as we need them."

Before playing around with "what ifs" about my book, our dream adventure was always to go to Africa one summer and change our lives forever through helping special needs children and their families.

This will actually always be at the top of my vision board. When the kids were little, I was very involved in the pubic school system. Some days I wished I had gone to college to be a special education teacher. Heck, I was a substitute teacher for seven years and was PTA president for six years at my children's elementary school–with the hopes of making teaching my profession some day.

After my kids started getting older, I soon realized that this was what I had done to be as close as possible to my children and still work. However, going back to school in nursing was what I truly always wanted for myself. Even though, if I stop and think about it, there is nothing on this green earth makes me feel more loved than being in a classroom with children.

To stand before children in a classroom, smiling, communicating, and teaching, that was my happy place. I always started their day with positive words and ended their day with positive words. I was always teaching them that they could make a difference–no matter their size.

Most of the kids knew me as Eddie and Emily's mom. However, a lot of children only knew me as a substitute. When I would sub, I would always begin the teacher's lesson plans after we had used our imagination a little bit.

I would stand at the front of the class, quietly saying, "Clap once if you can hear me." Eventually they would become as still as ice sculptures, wondering what was I clapping about. (Now, usually this only worked in third grade down.) I would pull down from the air my imaginary "thinking cap." After I put it onto my head just right, I would pretend to tuck my hair into the cap and tie the ribbon in a pretty bow under my chin. I would stand and mime in an imaginary mirror, smiling at my reflection, waiting for them to respond.

Then, I would gesture for them to do the same. They delighted in this activity. Some kids used to pretend their cap got away and had floated to the ceiling. I would jump up to get it for them. However, if not handled correctly, in a flash they would all be out of their seats, jumping with me!

I would walk the rows of the desks, complimenting everyone on their thinking caps as I passed out scrap paper to each child, inviting them to write their positive word for the day. Everyone got a turn to read the word off his or her scrap paper. Every child was given a thumbs up or an air clap after sharing the word with the class. Not to show favoritism, I would collect their words and put them in a hat–usually my Dr. Seuss hat–and then I would pick five words randomly. I would write those five words on the chalkboard with great enthusiasm. The rule of these words was simple. Whenever someone used one of the words in a sentence throughout the morning, I would add one minute to the after-lunch recess time. Proudly, I have to say, we were always the last class in from lunch recess.

Still to this day, kids will come up to me and say a positive word they learned when I substituted. One kid just graduated, and I taught him in the second grade. He walked up to me at the grocery store just the other day and said, "Phenomenal," as he leaned in to hug me. I wore a spectacular smile for the rest of the day. Thinking to myself as I pushed the cart around the store, *Good job, Christine. That was ten years ago! Amazing!*

Every ounce of me still believes that if Emily and I had the resources, our hearts would be a powerful force to make things right for all children in Africa with special needs–or for any child without a voice for that matter. Drifting back to the kitchen table, I heard Emily talking to me.

"Yeah, Mom, cool. I know Julia would be all over that! You know, what would be better? If Julia were to read your book and *then* help us make this happen. Maybe she will invite us to her home because she believes in our house in Africa just as much as we do. We will hang out with her, sit with her in her family room, meet her kids, and get a tour of her totally cool un-Hollywood house, because Julia is famous, but her house is normal."

I was so excited with Emily's fantasy that I interrupted her, "Don't forget! We will be drinking iced tea prepared by Julia herself, prepared with delicious mint leaves from her very own garden!" I made "mmmm" sounds as I closed my eyes.

"I hate tea. Please, Mom, let *me* finish!" She paused because my interruption had messed up her thinking pattern.

"Oh, yeah," she began again. "Julia is talking to us while you are drinking your mint iced tea, and she begins telling us all about her last trip to Africa. Then she asks us to join her in her dinning room. Julia starts showing us an enormous map of Africa that she has already marked with possible locations for our special house. When she stops talking, she leans over and picks up her cell phone. She doesn't explain to us who she is calling. But, we don't care–it's Julia! Right, Mom?" Emily paused midstream in her talking.

"Mom, are you even listening?" She tapped the table in front of me. My eyes are closed to give her amazing story a picture in my mind.

"Am I listening? Emily, I am already there!" Still with my eyes closed, I grabbed an invisible iced tea in front of me and pretended to take a drink.

She continued, "Then we will hear Julia laugh and say, 'Hey, George, it's me. Do you have a second? I have two very special people here, and we know you will want to be a part of this. We need a donation for a project you will loooove!' Then she turns to us and winks. She begins to tell George all about our house for children with special needs. She will give us a nod as she points to her phone. Julia will give us a huge smile and a thumbs up, as if to say, 'Oh, yes, ladies! It is *the* George Clooney!' And, Mom, he says, 'YES!'"

HEARTS-LOVE-CANCER 4

"Oh, come on! I swear this office is haunted," I said to myself under my breath as I scurried along the dimly lit hallway to the work kitchen one morning. The office where I work was still asleep; no one else was around. Finding the switch, I quickly flipped on the lights. The instant glow and warming hum from above made me feel instantly comforted.

Every time I am in this office by myself, I get such a creepy feeling. It's like I am not alone, when I clearly am. I heard myself saying under my breath, "Whatever, Christine. You know it is just your mind working overtime!"

Lord knows I have watched my share of Steven King movies, and I have binged on too many ghost stories in the past. I am good at creating such ridiculous, spooky scenarios in my mind that I could probably even make a well-lit room appear haunted.

But, I could not shake the shivers or head-to-toe goose bumps. I stood and rubbed my arms, trying to warm myself up. At least once a day at work, I get an icy chill. It's like for a quick second I have stepped into a walk-in freezer.

Usually I blame the AC, not eating breakfast, or one of my kids or their free-loading friends for having dumped something viral on me. But, this day felt different. I saw the flickering lights and heard radios turn to static as I walked by. It drove me crazy. Not to mention, the doors propped open with a door wedge suddenly closed when I walked back by, not even twenty seconds later. Who knows? Maybe I was just tired on this particular morning; hell, I am always tired.

Although, a couple of months ago, my girlfriends and I did go to a psychic in Cassadaga. According to the Travel Channel, it's the most spiritual place in the U.S., or one of them anyway.

Well, there we all sat in a room that glowed in shades of flickering purple candlelight. To me, the room had a homey, but corny, feel to it. A little wrought iron table sat in the middle of the room. Pictures of women from varying decades lined the walls haphazardly. I can remember being very fidgety and feeling terrified with the thoughts of what I would be told. Plus, I had lost the coin toss between us. This meant I was to go first.

Madame Rayne "appeared" as if out of nowhere. She shook all our hands, asking us our names. I thought she was pretty normal looking. I think she was wearing every beaded necklace she owned. I don't know what I was expecting her to look like. Maybe I expected something like that psychic from years ago in the television commercials. *What was her name? Cleo, the psychic!* I started smiling that I remembered such a thing. Madame Rayne stopped dead in her tracks right in front of me. She turned only her head and looked at me, smiling. She reached out and took my hand, gesturing with her other hand for me to come to her table. She started saying my name, "Christine," emphasizing the *s* each time: "Chissssstine."

It was so spooky. Did she know I lost the coin toss? I tried to tell myself that the room must be bugged and that's why she picked me first. I stood up, reluctantly went to her table, and sat down across from her.

After several minutes of uncomfortable silence, she told me, "Chrisssstine, you, my dear, possess psychic abilities." She said it just like that. She blurted it out in a very matter-of-fact tone, like saying to me, "You have brown hair." It gave me the creeps!

While starring directly into my eyes, she took my right hand and laid it in hers. She leaned in–a little too close for my comfort–and asked me if I was aware of my beautiful and powerful aurora.

I remember making a joke, asking Madame Rayne if my aurora could produce a money tree in my backyard. Then, I reconsidered, thinking that maybe my crass, smartass humor would not help me out right now–or get her to tell me what I wanted to hear. *What did I want to hear anyways?*

She stared at me, in a non-threatening way, rubbing my palm. My girlfriends had guzzled down too many "spirits," so to speak, and could not stop laughing behind me. She couldn't have cared less what they were doing behind us; her concentration was absolutely amazing.

She continued with a few generic things, about my life line, things like that. She ended with, "Chrissssstine, you must keep your mind open. It will all fall into place. It will come to you. Your wonderful gifts and abilities will find their way to your heart. Do you understand me?" I just found myself nodding in silence with my mouth hanging open.

"Chrissssstine, your gifts are something we dream about seeing here. We wait for women like you to walk through this door." All I could muster up was, "Oh, cool." I tried to get up, but started to fumble around with the little wire chair because the legs got stuck on the carpet. This sent my friends behind me into a cackling-hyena kind of laughter. I just went over to the wall, sat down, and rubbed my right hand. I was trying not to think of what she told me moments ago, but I kept wondering, *If she is so psychic, what were these gifts? Why couldn't she just tell me? Complete phony,* I said to myself.

Leaving my thoughts with Madame Rayne, I brought my mind back to the office and decided to unpack my lunch box and make some of the tea I brought from home. I found myself transfixed by the wall that stood before me. It is laced with beautiful canvas hearts I painted.

Listening to the hum of the microwave behind me, I blurted out to the hearts all hanging there, "Good morning, everyone!" My heartfelt smile transformed my worries of spirits and ghosts to thoughts of love. My body instantly started to warm up.

I started painting the canvases when I lost my first patient to cancer. My unbearable heartache was devastating. I did not know how to process it. Healthcare workers are supposed to be tough, to be the anchors for the patient and family. I am this rock while I am at work. But at home, when the night is quiet and I am all tucked in, I sometimes find my mind won't stop thinking of how I won't get to see the patient anymore. I am happy he or she is pain free, but tearful of my loss.

We spend so much time with our patients that I decided to pay tribute to the unconditional love they gave us. I would not forget what each went through or allow a unique life to become just another patient. Releasing my sadness through creativity and art is as natural for me as a duck is to water.

Some hearts I have painted are with watercolors; some are with oils; some are with pastels; and some are with craft paint. A few of them have sequins; some have poems; and some have glitter. Some hearts have all of those elements combined. There are twelve hearts on our wall, all added in the year and a half I have been here.

Each heart that is on our Wall of Hearts is unique to a particular patient. I paint what I feel about the patient, not what I see. We keep them displayed on the wall in our kitchen, at the request of the doctor. I get it. They would draw a lot of attention. Why? Because they are amazing little works of art. At first, I was a little pissed that he wanted to keep them out of sight and hidden. But, when you are fighting the fight, they still represent someone we lost to the fight.

They really stir emotions for those who do see them. One time a drug rep came to set up lunch in our kitchen. She was so drawn to this wall that she came up to our desk area and asked me, "Christine, I don't remember seeing these hearts last time. What do they mean?" She looked so sad when I told her I would be back in thirty minutes to explain.

There she sat waiting, sitting dead center in front of the wall in a little folding chair with her legs crossed and her hands folded in her lap, just smiling and taking in each brush stroke. As I explained to her the meaning behind each canvas and why I started doing this, she never once mentioned the drug she was there to promote. She just shared the story of how her mother died of cancer and said she wanted a heart. Could I please paint her mother a heart?

After a dear patient passes, we always invite family and friends back to see the tribute I made. When they see the special little canvas I created for their loved one, so many hugs and tears of happiness are exchanged. Hearing me explain each brush stroke and what they truly represent often leaves the family speechless.

Most ask if they can have a moment alone with their heart, after asking me if they can photograph it. Promising me, even though I didn't ask them too, that they will take my story of love and share it with as many people as they can. I feel so privileged each time I get to share my masterpiece with someone–not because I spend days making them, but because I really think about the person it represents. I paint each canvas with the particular patient on my mind. I even say a prayer for each person before I begin, and I stop if my mind gets distracted. It's a labor of love that I feel privileged to take on.

No other comparison seems suitable to describe what our patients go through other than ridding one hell-of-a-scary roller coaster ride. From the very first visit, when I meet my new patient in the waiting room, we hold hands as I welcome them. I want to symbolize togetherness, that we will be on this ride together.

As the coaster starts to progress on its track, the ride always begins with the click, click, click of the gears grinding, taking them up to that first crest, that first plunge, that first monster hill. Sometimes, depending on where you are sitting on this coaster, you may have to hang over this ominous first hill and wait for the back end to gain momentum and catch up. You may have to wait for that stomach-in-your-mouth, agonizing first drop. It is an earth-shaking, vibrating plummet into the unknown. Cancer! It's just like a coaster ride.

Some patients, as they get on this cancer coaster, put their hands up ready for the challenge! Like, "Woo-hoo I got this! This cancer won't get me!" Some others cover their eyes or bury their heads in the armpit of whomever is sitting next to them. Some hyperventilate; some throw up. Some scream up to the sky, shouting, "Lord, please let me off, and please turn this ride around!" Some just start stomping and crying. Some are frozen with fear, and it takes days to talk about "it."

That first hill is like grasping that you have cancer. Next comes the hellacious spinning loops as you get a clear understanding of the cancer you have and what chemo you will take. Then there are more thundering drops and dark, looming tunnels as the chemo is now pumping through your body; it has left your white blood cell count at zero. You begin to ask, "Will germs kill me before the cancer? Will I survive this?" Zooming blindly up the track to take on more terrifying twists and tortuous turns, you are greeted by the horrible side effects of chemo: hair is falling out; you have fever, chills, vomiting, mouth sores, and endless insomnia. Flying through more upside down loops and strobe-light-flashing tunnels, there are more PET scans, CT scans, and blood transfusions.

Sometimes patients get to move safely to the home-base terminal. Finally, they can take off that shoulder harness and unbuckle the seatbelt. They get off this exhausting and treacherous ride because yes, hallelujah, the chemotherapy worked, and the ride is over!

Some patients have to speed right through that home-base terminal and get on this chemo-cancer coaster again and again and again. They hear that the tumor has grown, the chemo is not working, or the cancer has spread to another organ.

I ride this coaster with hopeful pride, every single day. Sometimes I ride along eight or nine times a day, depending on how many patients are visiting me. I am always ready to ride, no matter how many times the patient has had to challenge this coaster. I believe deep down in my soul that someday we can sit on a real amusement park bench together, holding hands, breathing softly, and knowing he or she doesn't have to ride the cancer coaster ever, ever again.

Maybe we can even enjoy a frozen chocolate-covered banana and smile about the future again. I want to look out at this coaster with my patient, my friend, my now family, and gush with pride at his courageous bravery facing the coaster ride. I want to take a picture of him or her wearing an "I survived the cancer coaster" t-shirt!

I get attached to every single patient. In nursing school, it is drilled into your head: do NOT get attached. Getting involved is completely taboo. They are just patients; treat them with kindness and respect, but never cross the line. You are just to treat the problem, not the person. I actually think that philosophy is what's wrong with healthcare today.

Well, I guess I am not normal–thank the Lord–because I just can't do that. Maybe it's that I lack the genetic makeup to keep my distance. My DNA just does not have this switch. Besides, how can I *not* get involved? My patients become my family. I always, always keep this question in the back of my mind: how would I want my mother to be treated, or my sister, my daughter, my son, my husband, or my brother? Needless to say, the problem, ugh, drives me crazy just thinking about it!

As a matter of fact, I was a pistol in nursing school, always challenging my instructor. I exasperated her. But, when I graduated with honors and the highest GPA in my class, she finally softened for me. She came up to me at graduation and said in her very thick Boston accent, "Christine, you will go far; keep that moxie! Okay?" We just stood there laughing, hugging each other, and knowing *that* would not be a problem!

Some days I could never figure out why the good Lord picked me up and dropped me in Orange City, Florida. All the jobs I have had through my life are, whoa, too many to dive into right now. I usually felt like I was on the Island of Misfit Toys in the working world. I always felt empty–unless I was working with children in a classroom. That is, of course, until I found this doctor's office, until I found the door that led me here.

Cancer is really as ugly and sinister as you might think. Often, others say to me, "Of all the ways to spend your day, you chose *that*? I just couldn't do it. How do you do it?" If only I had a dollar for every time I have heard those questions, I am pretty sure I could make a big financial contribution in helping to find a cure.

Cancer has opened my eyes. It has shaken up my safe little existence and made me see through different lenses. The "C word" has helped me understand the grand scheme of life, which is actually quite simple: Live everyday as if you were given a gift, as if it were your last. Be conscious of what you say, how you act, and keep in the back of your mind the question, "Did I make a difference?"

Now do I still have bad days or pity-party days? Of course! I am human. But, this journey and loving my patients through the ins and outs of their disease has taught me more than I could have imagined.

Cancer couldn't care less about how much money you have in the bank or how much you earn in a year. Cancer does not care what kind of car you drive or what your address is. Cancer does not care if you have health insurance or not. It doesn't care if you are a newlywed or a new mother. It doesn't care that you just retired and are planning a once-in-a-lifetime vacation. Cancer does not give a crap about your age, what color your skin is, or if you worship Allah or Jesus. Cancer does not pick someone because of horrible acts, nor are you absolved for any righteous acts. Cancer has no boundaries, no limits, and no prejudices.

My goal is to piss cancer off every single day! How? By just being the same old me. Really! I believe that, along with medicine, if there are no walls up for me, no limits in allowing my heart to ever be judge or jury, I am taking a positive step in pissing cancer off! I will exhaust you, cancer! I will guard my patients like Fort Knox from the worry you want to plague them with! Cancer, you are the only poison. I will help my patients focus on destroying you and you alone!

I will have no prejudices whatsoever, and then my patients will know, believe, and feel that this office, this small space they come to day after day, can be a true refuge for healing. Cancer is the only enemy in my eyes–not my patients' past or their present. I strive to truly cherish and value their future, believing someday, together, we can beat this disease!

Sure, what I may learn about someone may sting from time to time. But, if I can let go of my anger when I see a man walk through our door covered in head-to-toe KKK tattoos, I sure as hell have outsmarted cancer! I've done this, not by looking the other way, but by taking this person's heart and giving it new energy, a fresh beginning, a day filled with genuine hope and pure love. I honestly strive to be the change I wish to see in the world. Believe me, a heart is more powerful than people give it credit.

I have witnessed healing from the inside out. Day after day, I am witness to the beauty of a heart. The heart is mystical and unique, just like a snowflake. All are completely different. There is not one heart that loves, thinks, beats, or bleeds the same.

How did I get so lucky? I am a girl who has spent half of her life on a quest to understand the true meaning of love.

Something as ugly as cancer taught me about love?

Amazing!

GIFT 5

S am, a patient, once told me, "I've never met someone like you before!" He said I was an anomaly, a gift of joy to him and his spirit. He said I changed his life. I believe he changed mine forever, too.

The two of us were sitting quietly in the exam room, waiting for the doctor to come in, when he asked if he could share something with me. I didn't hesitate, "Of course, please." This was a very easy response for me.

"Christine, I believe that my cancer is my punishment," he said to me as he rolled to his side on the exam table to face me. Silent tears were making his shirt collar wet.

I went over and got the rolling chair so I could sit down and be on eye level with him. Taking his hand in mine, all I said was, "Go on."

"You know, I was a cop for the NYPD. Well, I shot a man once and took his life. This cancer is what I call 'an eye for an eye.'"

I never took my gaze off him as I just breathed in and out. I replied, "You know, I cannot imagine your pain. But, you must let go of this. That guilt you are carrying is eating you up. You and I both know guilt is a useless emotion. Your cancer is hoping you won't let go of this regret and anger. It's praying you stay angry at everything but your cancer." Sam reached out to me and took my hand; he leaned in very close.

In a whisper tone, just for the two of us, I continued, "Sam, it is feeding on your sorrow. I want you to ask yourself this: what did the nine-year-old I met this past weekend at the Ronald McDonald House do to get cancer of the blood?" We locked eyes. I let him absorb what I was saying.

He instantly started weeping and sobbing and holding me tightly. The doctor, having heard the gut-wrenching sobs, came flying in the room. He said, "Christine?" as he held his hands palm up to ask, what's going on?

Sam quickly let the doctor know that it was just time for him to cry and that they were tears of relief. The doctor nodded to both of us and quietly shut the door.

The doctor knows that our patients tell me everything. At first, I think it drove him nuts, but after a while, he realized I do not solicit or seek anything from people. They just naturally share stuff with me.

Snapping out of my memory trance, I found myself still in the in the office's lunchroom. I stopped and smiled at all my wonderful hearts on the wall.

Deciding to leave while my thoughts are on love, I take my warm tea to my computer, and I flick on the screen to see what kind of day lies ahead.

I see my sweet patient is coming in! I am so, so happy that I will see her! Her battle with cancer has been a two-trip coaster ride for her so far, my sweet Claudia.

I love to go out of my way and talk with our patients about anything other than cancer or the chemo drug they are taking. They get enough of those discussions in the real world.

I love sharing normal things, like what's on sale at the grocery store, or something as simple as where the new traffic light is going up in town. I might talk about a new restaurant I tried, a great movie I just watched, or the latest feel-good story on the news.

I also share lots of anecdotes about the domestic bliss I go home to. My growing teens and their adventures keep everyone laughing. Patients also ask where my husband is now. They ask because he drives a truck over the road and is gone a lot. My one patient tells me every time I see him that if Jimmy Hoffa was still alive, the Teamsters would have taken better care of me and my family, and I would not have to work. He makes me laugh with his old-school ways.

It is the little nuances that can become interesting all of the sudden. This is especially true when your focus becomes mouth sores, hair falling out, aching bones, weight loss, vomit, and fatigue so severe that you daydream about actually sleeping.

One day I took Claudia back to the little makeshift library I set up in the office. After her second cycle of chemo and radiation at the age of seventy-six, she told me she was tired of lying around the house waiting to feel better.

I began handing her book after book. Eventually, she said to me, "Well, I can't see too well anymore, and I don't know the last book I finished." I take her cue that books are not her thing.

"Okay, how about a movie?" I said, smiling and handing her a couple VHS tapes.

"I think my son and daughter-in-law gave me a tape player for these things years ago. I don't think I ever took it out of the box." She stood there staring at the tapes like I do when I open a road map, completely lost.

"Well, tell your son to get over to your house and show you how to use it! I have a ton of them, see?" Holding my hands up with flare to show her all of the ancient tapes behind me, I gave her my best Vanna White impression.

Before long, she was hooked. She soon loved to share with me the latest movie she had watched. One day, she was happy to tell me that I reminded her of an actress. I had created quite the movie critic.

"You know what? You remind me of this sweet girl in a movie I just watched, Christine. You know, the movie with the girl who lives in the South? She is a little chubbier, but she is a spitfire like you! In the movie, she is married to an Ed, too!" I was thinking to myself, *Gee, thanks.*

Claudia knows I have a weird, Jeopardy-competition-worthy mind with movies. I can usually recall a movie when someone recites just one line. However, this one had me stumped. Plus, I was trying to get my mind to shake off the word *chubby*.

There she sat. With a bright pink do-rag on her bald head. But, she was smiling so big! She eagerly waited while I tried to think of whom she was talking about, helping her to escape the doctor's office into the world of film.

"Is she gorgeous, with a head for business and a bod for sin?" I asked her, trying really hard not to crack up laughing, thinking to myself how cool Melanie Griffith's character was in *Working Girl.*

Claudia had just finished watching *Working Girl,* which she loved and talked about for weeks. It had taken me about that long to convince her to watch it. I had to promise her it was not about a prostitute and that I would never recommend something like that.

Damn. I forgot about Pretty Woman!

"I love that movie!" she started to chuckle. She loved to tell me that I made her feel young again.

"Come on, Ms. Christine, the woman in this movie that reminds me of you is best friends with the main character from that Driving Around Miss Daisy movie. Oh, you know it! I see it on your face!" she said, giggling.

I did know it. I suddenly knew she was talking about *Friend Green Tomatoes.*

"Towanda! Oh, my stars, you mean Evelyn!" I was now speaking in my best southern twang, which had her laughing and pointing at me.

"Yes, you remind me of her. I think I am going to watch that movie a couple more times before I bring it back. I enjoyed that picture! You can always guess what I am talking about. I may need to call you from the grocery store if I forget my list. I bet you would know what I needed. I seem to forget what I did not even five minutes ago!" She was looking at me with the biggest smile. I found myself grinning from ear to ear.

As I took Claudia's vital signs, I fell silent thinking, *Kathy Bates, huh? Why didn't I remind her of a statuesque Sigourney Weaver from* Working Girl? *Oh, hell, Kathy is awesome! I suppose I could use some hormones, like the character Evelyn in the movie.*

I tried to cover my grin, for fear she would think I was snickering at her and not the actresses in my mind. Then she piped up and said, wagging her finger at me, "You know, Christine, don't you laugh! Life really does go by with a blink of an eye. Poof! Your memory is gone! I, however, do not forget what it was like being younger. Oh, Christine, to be twenty six again and young, my Heavens!" She held her lower back as she struggled to stand up.

"What do you remember most about being young?" I asked her, holding my hand down and twirling my index finger, gesturing for her to turn around so I could retie her pink bandana on her head.

Without hesitation, she said, "Oh, I miss my hair! When I was younger, I had long, beautiful auburn hair. My grandmother used to rip up old pillowcases and wrap my hair up to make curls. You know, she called it rag rolls. Oh, those curls! They had the perfect bounce!" She paused, and the sweetest sounding sigh left her mouth–almost like when you take a bite of a warm glazed donut.

I spun her around by her shoulders so that she faced me again. She instantly looked up at me and grinned through glistening eyes.

"You know, I can picture you with those curls! Wow! You *did* have amazing hair!" I told her, as I pretended to bounce her curls on the palms of my hands.

"Yes, yes, I told you! I was a real catch, you know. I could have had any young man's hand with my good looks!" She grinned up at me as she fluffed and bounced her pretend curls too.

"I bet you also looked outa this world in the color yellow, with your skin coloring and that auburn hair! Hello! Woo-hoo, knockout!" My eyes began to fill with tears, and my throat had that unbearable, pre-cry sting.

Still facing each other, she took both of my hands and said, "And, don't you forget it!" Then she winked at me, allowing her tears to roll softly down her cheeks. Not letting go of my hands, she squeezed me even more tightly.

"Never! I could never, ever forget," I said as my voice trailed off. I bowed my head, understanding what we were really talking about. Every fiber in my heart was aching, overflowing with sadness. I began desperately pleading with my mind, *Do not start crying, Christine. Not now.* But tears were already fluttering down my cheeks.

"Oh, come on now; we can't stand here and cry! You haven't even tried my pumpkin bread I made you." She reached in her tote and pulled out a semi-warm loaf wrapped in plastic wrap. She had tied it with a green cloth bow.

I said to her in my best southern drawl, "Oh, my goodness! You are really naughty! You know my weakness is anything made with pumpkin! I am going to eat the whole thing by noon and get so fat!" She linked arms with me and patted her hand on my arm; we both quickly wiped our tears away, as if we hadn't been crying.

"Well, I am not so sure about that; you know, I made it from memory. We'll see if you like it." She was chuckling through her sniffles as I pretend to look worried and reluctantly took the bread from her hands.

I stopped the act and reassured her, "I can promise every bite will end with MmmmmMmmmmMmmm!" The two of us started really laughing at my exaggerated *Mmmmm* sounds.

We continued walking down the long hall to her chair, her room for the day, to get her hooked up to receive her daily regimen of chemo. She talked the whole way with a new smile. She told me all about how her mother used to have bee hives, just like that little girl Idgie in *Fried Green Tomatoes*. She said that in her hometown in Georgia, there was a café exactly like the one in the movie.

As she got nestled down in her chair, she told me how her mother would have loved me, how in some ways I reminded her of her mother, and how she can tell I have a very old soul.

Getting her all set up, with her pillows and blanket she brought from home–along with her water bottle and her giant box of tissues–I leaned down and kissed her on the top of her head. She reached up and held my cheek in her hand. Without hesitation, she said to me, "I love you," and then closed her eyes.

I stopped in the doorway and waved to her. I blew her a kiss, which she caught and held in a closed fist next to her face. I felt that chill again. This was the first time I had seen her with her eyes closed. She looked so depleted, so frail, so tired from riding the continuous cancer coaster, my dear, sweet Claudia.

She said, while smiling, peeking through one eye, and waving her tissue at me, "Now, go. Get back to work! Stop fussing over me. I am so tired. I need to take a rest! Go on. Shoo!"

Making my way around the corner, out of sight from anyone in the office, I found a private corner and rested my forehead against the wall. I supported all my weight on my throbbing, pounding head. Clutching my pumpkin bread close to my chest, I stood still, only listening to my breathing. Alone, I felt hundreds of tears slide off my cheeks and chin, quietly dripping to the ground below. All of me knew what was coming for Claudia.

I knew it was time to prepare my broken heart–and a new canvas heart for our wall.

SERIOUSLY?

6

That night after work, I realized there was not a single thing to throw together for dinner in the fridge, so I decided to drive past my turn home and head to the grocery store.

Still feeling completely drained from all the holiday cheer, I was waiting for my new calendar year to begin with fresh hope and all that my horoscope invited me to enjoy in 2013. I sat in my van in the packed parking lot. I felt like a puddle with eyeballs, and I let out a huge sigh. Was working with cancer patients draining me away?

I decided to text each of my teens to tell them I was stopping at store, getting dinner, and heading home in fifteen minutes. "Do not leave until I get home," I instructed.

As I sat in the van, desperately wishing I owned a magic wand that would magically allow groceries to appear in my back seat, my kids started firing texts back to me: "Please get me some hair gel. What did you decide to make for dinner? Did you have a good day?"

My daughter's text ended with multiple smiley faces and tons of *ox*'s.

On the other hand, my son's text was a bit different: "What disgusting and gross dinner are you making us eat now? I thought I told you to get me some deodorant. Where is it?" I felt the heat rising and found myself saying out loud, "Breathe."

For my own sanity, I decided not to text either back. Plus, what I wanted to text my son probably should not be in print form ever.

I just sat, staring at a blank piece of paper, holding a pen, and making little square boxes all over it instead of a list. I was telling myself, *Come on, Chris, Try to throw some sort of list together before you enter the packed store. You will be sorry if you don't write something down!* I was wishing I had bought groceries for more than two meals when I shopped a couple of days ago. I know better than to go shopping on a Monday.

Whenever I go to the grocery store after work, especially on a Monday, my mind is usually still buzzing from work. I have what I call "mush brain," which makes me buy random things, like hand soap, bananas, and paper plates. I go home to a very confused family that is looking for food to form a meal. I insist, "You told me we were out of hand soap. Yes, you did!"

Instead of making a list, I gazed out my van window and watched a homeless man very intently. He is shaking so noticeably that even his dog has his head cocked to the side, looking worried too. The leash the old guy is holding is swinging like he is trying to jump rope.

I love to people watch. I wish they actually had a degree in people watching. I suppose that's probably an elective you can take if you are entering the FBI or something. To me, people are fascinating: their mannerisms, facial expressions, what they say, what they are wearing, and how they interact with each other is unique and surprising.

Lord, take me to an amusement park, get me a shady bench, and come back in two hours. You will find me completely content, not even fussing about how long you have been gone. I can sit and watch people until the cows come home. Actually, I usually tell my family, "What? You are back already?"

This guy had obviously been homeless for quite some time. The gear he was carrying indicated that he knew what he was doing on the streets. I saw him reach over and detach the blanket that was strapped to his duffel bag. He shook it out, laid it down, and began to smooth it out, making sure each corner was nice and flat.

Awe, I suddenly realized he was doing this for his dog! He patted the blanket for her to come over and lie down. She did as instructed; as she settled down, she looked completely pooped out. *It must have been a long day of walking for the two of them*, I thought to myself as I leaned into the dash a little more to get a better view.

He clips her leash to a very heavy-looking backpack, takes out a water bowl, and goes over to the faucet on the wall of the grocery store to fill the big bowl to the top with water.

The whole time, his hands were shaking as he held the bowl. He had pretty good skills, and it looked like he was used to his hands shaking. He moved to the right and left, not dropping an inch of water anywhere. He sat the water bowl down, surprisingly gingerly. With some struggle in getting up, she came over and started lapping up the delicious, fresh water.

My eyes began to tear up, and all I could think was, *This is the nicest thing I have seen all day. They are a family.* He waited until she was done getting her fill of water and back on her tattered but smooth blanket. He stroked her head a few times, told her something, and headed off into the store.

My phone started wildly buzzing and humming in my hand, still on vibrate from being at work. Looking down at my phone, I realized I had nine missed texts from my kids. *It's been all of five minutes, and they have texted me nine more times*, I thought as I scrolled through them.

"Are you there!!!!!!" My son.

"???" My son.

"Are you going to get me some hair gel? Please?" More smiley faces. My daughter.

"I don't want to eat whatever slop you are making!!!" My son.

"I need gas money; can you get me ten bucks cash back?" My son.

"Whatever you get, I am good with it. I didn't eat any lunch!" My daughter.

Just smiley faces. My daughter.

Taking Katie for a little walk down the street. Okay? My daughter.

WTF? My son.

I was so caffeine deprived that I didn't know if I had the energy to respond to the texts, let alone walk around the grocery store. I finally decided just to get it over with, and I shot some texts back to each of them, hoping to end the text war.

"Hi, Emily. I am bringing fried chicken home, and yes to your gel. Thank you for all your smileys. I love you and will see you in fifteen minutes. Today was a good day at work. Hope your day at school was nice; we'll talk all about it when I get home. Love you!" Smiley faces.

"Hi, son. Your deodorant is on your dresser. Eat if you want. Up to you. I am bringing fried chicken home. You may borrow ten bucks, but I want it back. Don't ever, I repeat, ever swear to me–even if it's in a text. EVER! Be home in fifteen minutes. I love you."

My son did not respond, but my daughter sent me about twenty more smileys, all with different smiles. I found myself smiling, too. Telling myself to practice what I preach, I thought of what I tell the kids: *Make it a great day or not; the choice is yours.*

Why is my son so angry? Everyone assures me it's the age. Bullshit. I am tired of him being so nasty to me. He is always nice, though, if he wants something. Sounds familiar. I remember being the same as him when I was a kid.

Damn. Note to self: call mom and dad; apologize for all of it!

Once in the store, I found the fluorescent lights almost nauseating. Trying my very best to stay focused and move at lightning speed up and down the isles–despite my should-have-been-retired-months-ago shopping cart–I realized I never made a list. I ordered myself, *You must keep hair gel at the top of your mind. Focus, focus! You can do it! Christine, do not forget hair gel.*

Suddenly, I saw *her* in my peripheral vision. I began shivering with worry that she would spot me! *Oh, Lord, she will go on and on and on about how great her kids are, which takes an eternity.* I don't even have to ask or utter a single question for her to begin the litany.

Why? Why do I always run into her at this grocery store? Every time, it is the same. She starts what I call diarrhea of the mouth. She never will even ask how my kids are doing, and our kids have known each other since they were four years old.

When she would call and ask if our sons could get together and have a sleep over, I would tell my son, "No, you can't go over to his house to spend the night. You felt warm earlier. I think you are getting sick. Sorry, buddy."

Horrible! Just awful, I know. But, it was never just a matter of letting my son out at the door to spend the night. She would be waiting for me to pull in her driveway. Even if you said, "Nah, I really got to be getting back home," she would respond, "Oh, come on, just a short visit." I would always cave, thinking, okay, she is taking my kid for the night; I can do just a short visit.

But it was always the same. I would sit in her very small family room, on a very small love seat, usually next to a giant-sized bag of lawn fertilizer. I would be forced to eat taco dip her mother-in-law made before she went to work. The dip looked like her very hairy, very drooly dog (which was fascinated with cramming its snout in your crotch) had chewed up and spit back into the lopsided and extremely stained Tupperware. Ugh!

Not to mention, she was a photographer, and you better have the stamina to look at every picture she took for the last decade. They were all different poses of her delightful dynamos, starting with the year they were born. And you better not blink, because Lord help you if you missed one. Missing one photo means you must rewind the whole CD, and you start back at the beginning.

I would usually rate the pros and cons of making up a fake story to get out of there. I would actually start praying to the Lord in my mind, *Forgive me, Lord, for I am about to lie. Now, Lord, this is not going to be the usual white lie. This will be a whopper of a lie. Have mercy, Lord. I will be asking for forgiveness in about five minutes. Amen.*

The only way I would let Eddie spend the night there was if Ed was home and off the road. I would make him do sleepover drop-off. This brought him back exhausted, pissed, and usually mumbling under his breath about all we do for these kids.

Her kids are a mess, too. But, Heaven help you if you bring up the bad stuff about her precious little gems. I wish I had the balls to say, "Like, didn't your son get a girl pregnant when she was fifteen? Or, is your daughter still wishing she was a vampire?"

But nooooo. I just stand there in a daze, listening while she shares her titillating rendition (note my sarcasm) of how her son made first tuba. She will even tell you, in great detail, about the eight emails his music teacher sent on what a prodigy her son is with music. Or, she will talk about how her daughter was in love and had finally found her counterpart, her soulmate, the best reflection of her dream man. Then, in the very next sentence, she will say, "But, his mother is a nasty bitch whore, whom I despise!"

Really, she says stuff like this! It's almost like she has this ready-to-go loop she practices in her head when she might run into someone. Gag! Please don't let her see me!

She does and begins the expected dialogue about her kids, starting from half way across the store. I can literally hear the music from *The Wizard of Oz* playing in my own mind. You know the scene when the Wicked Witch is ridding her bike to get Toto? That!

All I could say, under my breath, was "Shit! Shit! Think. Think, Christine!" I literally felt my scrubs start to get wet under my armpits.

I waved to her like a lunatic, threw her an air kiss, and took off–only to hear her behind me. She had found someone else to share her kids' latest triumphs with.

Hair gel, juice, bread, toilet paper, and a twelve pack of diet coke. Lord, I am all over the store–one end to the other. I don't know why, either. You could blindfold me, tell me to go get five things, and I would find them.

Sometimes I will see customers asking a lost-looking employee where something is located. I just interrupt and tell the customer exactly where to find the item in question. Usually I intervene because I hear the untrained eighteen year old, with his cell phone in hand, responding, "Uh, we don't have those." Really, kid? You don't have toothpicks in a grocery store?

I wonder why that show *Supermarket Sweep* was cancelled. I always watched that show, knowing I would be the ultimate mega-shopper. I loved that show.

I finally found my way to the deli and grabbed an eight-piece box of chicken–all while trying to move stealth-like with my rickety cart. I was driven by fear of *you know who*! I was so completely panic-stricken that if I saw her, I might have screamed out, "Voldemort!"

I found myself chanting a mantra in my mind, *Please, please, please, gods of the grocery store, please hear me. Please have mercy, and don't let me round the corner and see her!*

When I finally got nestled into the checkout line, I let myself relax. Home free, I consoled myself by thinking that even if I run into her, I would be limited in conversation because I was sandwiched between two customers who were obviously in a hurry.

You know this type of grocery store regulars: toe-tapping, weight-shifting, and eye-rolling, holding all items in their hands. I don't know why this type always makes me laugh. I find their annoyance with waiting hysterical. I bet these are the same people that speed around you because you are going the speed limit. I love it when I catch up to them at the red light.

Sometimes, depending on my mood, I will look over at these annoyed drivers when we finally meet up again. I will let them catch my gaze, and then I throw my head back and laugh and laugh. I started to laugh in line, thinking to myself, *That's about it for my dangerous side.*

Up ahead of me by two people, I saw the homeless man from outside. He was slowly checking out and still shaking from head to toe.

I squeezed myself as close as I could get to the guy in front of me, trying not to appear too odd. His over-the-shoulder stare told me it was too late to avoid odd, but I wanted to hear what the old hag in front of him was saying.

I know. I didn't know her from Adam, but this hag seemed kind of rough. She was making a stink, and trust me, you don't have to hear what someone is saying to know when they are making a stink about something.

She was pointing her chubby finger at the phone next to the register, telling the very confused checkout kid to "call the manager to open another checkout line, NOW!"

The homeless man was now shaking uncontrollably. His change, apparently collected from his long day of begging, was popping out of his white hanky and rolling all over the conveyer belt, disappearing to the floor as the belt kept moving.

Over the scratchy, fuzzy, and way-too-loud loud speaker, I could hear from above that the kid being bullied by chubby fingers was saying, "Gary, can you, like, come to register two? Like, now? Please, man."

The kid obviously didn't realize his microphone was still on. After he was done calling Gary up to the front of the store, I could hear his shallow breathing and gum chewing for about twenty more seconds.

I started laughing out loud, which made every head snap back at me, looking at me like, one more noise, lady, and we will personally walk you to the cauldron of grocery store doom!

The guy in front of me stepped out of line to wait and see which new line the manager, Gary, would come and open.

The woman with the fat arms and sausage fingers started waving over an innocent bag boy, who looked at her, completely terrified.

Through her snout, she huffed at him, "Don't just stand there, you idiot! Pick up my stuff and take it over to the manager. He can ring up my groceries! This BUM is taking up my precious time!" She was speaking about the homeless man as if he were a very gross wad of gum she was trying to scrape off her shoes.

"Unreal!" I found myself saying out loud so she could hear. I know myself; I was teetering on the brink of a real freak out.

I squeezed past my cart and left my groceries. I went up behind this man, put my hand on his shoulder, and smiled to him. He turned to me and smiled back, wiping his chin on his shoulder as he turned his head back and bowed it to the floor. I noticed veteran patches and stars on his jacket.

Then, I snapped my head over to the marshmallow peep in a housecoat, and we had a glaring standoff. I think to myself, *What is wrong with this lady? His service for our Country kept her free to behave like this? Lady, you unearthed my crazy! Take your pork and beans to the manager. GO!*

This is what played through my mind as I stared at her. My glare must have been intimidating because she finally looked away. I felt somewhat victorious! I was taking it "old school" at the Winn Dixie.

The checkout clerk was getting frustrated at the possible scolding from Gary, so he told the homeless guy, "Look, man, you don't have enough money," in an I-couldn't-care-less kind of tone.

I reached out to the guy holding his hanky full of change and gently closed it with my own hand. Looking down, I saw one giant bottle of rose wine and a single serving of steak-n-cheese dog food.

I tried my very best not to displace my anger on Brett, the checkout guy, and to let go of my big attitude and staring contest with pork and beans, who was now in checkout line three.

"Sir, may I pay for your groceries?" I asked, sounding like a squeaking bird. I was afraid I was going to end crying on this poor guy, still shocked at the way he had been treated.

"Look. Is one of you going to pay for it or what?" Brett said, as he yawned and started taking the red *paid for* stickers off the roll, sticking them all over the pole he was resting on.

"Brett. Is that your name?" I leaned into his personal space to make a point, squinting and darting my eyes back and forth between his name tag, and his face. He didn't say a word; he just yawned and stretched again, as if were at home in his bed, not at work.

"You, Brett, will bend down and pick up this man's change off the floor. You will then, Brett, wrap this up nicely in plastic," I commanded, handing him the jug of wine. "Then, Brett, you will bag it in a nice paper bag. Okay, Brett?" I was simultaneously trying to calculate how much money I had in my own account until Wednesday.

Brett couldn't have cared less what I told him. He rolled his eyes with great exaggeration as he bent down. He did pick up the coins, one at a time, and gently placed them back into the man's hand. The man said not one word, but something told me he was enjoying Brett's performance as much as I was.

Handing lazy Brett groceries I might not be able to afford until payday, I quickly scanned the cart with my eyes: chicken, hair gel, dog food, and wine. I kept thinking, *The last thing I need is to be humiliated in front of Brett because my debit card won't go through.* After some quick math, I found myself very happy; I will be okay.

The man took his wine and dog food and turned to me. He gave me a kind of bow. He didn't say a word, nor did I. But we didn't need to. Besides, that's not what I wanted. I did not want him to thank me for buying his stuff. It was more important to give this man his dignity–even if dumbass Brett didn't get it.

"Brett, you forgot my ten dollars in cash, please," I said, merrily holding my palm out to him. He let out the biggest sigh, like he just crossed the finish line at a decathlon.

"Come on, Brett, two more seconds and I will be out of your hair. Can you give me a smile, please*?"* He looked at me like he could kick himself for not taking that job at Taco Bell.

I headed out of the store, feeling quite happy and proud of myself, when I felt my pocket vibrate again. Yep, looking down at my phone, I saw a new text.

"Please tell me you didn't forget my damn money. What's taking you so long?" My son.

Racing my cart to the exit of the grocery store, I started looking to find the old man with the dog. It was almost as if my body knew what I was up to before my mind did.

"Excuse me, sir?" I shouted out, trying to catch up to the guy. I don't think in a million years he would expect someone to call after him; this is probably why he didn't stop.

I went over to his blanket and the little camp he had set up. His dog came right up to me and started licking my hands.

"Sir, I wanted to give you this," I said quickly as I held out the ten-dollar bill to him.

From his seated position, he didn't move. He shook his head, like lady, I get it; you have done enough.

He doesn't understand that this will be the best thing I could possibly teach my son in the eighteen years of raising him.

"Please, it's for dog food. I have two dogs myself; I know how much they eat." Deciding to still hold out my ten dollar bill, I didn't move or say another word.

He actually started smiling. Then he got up, took off his hat, and reached out to take the money. He started to say something, but I just put my hand up, as if to say, *Nope, it's okay.* This gesture made him smile more brightly.

He started petting his dog on the head and said in a very smooth, almost country voice, "Yep, she's a good girl; she does eat a lot some days–that is, depending on how far we travel."

The two of us just stood there talking for about fifteen minutes about our dogs, the weather, and where he was from. It was such an easy conversation. It felt natural talking to this stranger, who was no longer a stranger to me. He was now tucked in my heart as Jack, the United States veteran, whom I thanked humbly for giving me my freedom.

Little side note: it will always, always be one of my best memories.

WHAT IN THE HECK? 7

That next Saturday, I woke up in a mood. When these moods happen, I often find I am even annoyed with myself. You know these moods, the kind where everything is just (ugh)! Nothing tastes good or looks appetizing, and even the spoons in your silverware drawer make you angry. And you find yourself saying things out loud like, "Why on earth did I buy these spoons?"

I finally thought to myself, *Forget it!* I went outside to soak up the fresh morning air, and I stood with my dog in the front yard, while she sniffed a thousand different spots to do her business. I said out loud, "What a gorgeous day to take a drive!"

I told my dog, "Sorry, you missed your opportunity; fifteen minutes was long enough to find a spot to pee!" I scooped her up and took her back inside. Spotting my keys, I thought to myself, *Okay, just a short drive around the block. Get rid of your nasty mood; it will do everyone some good—especially you, Christine!*

Backing down the driveway in my van, I saw my family looking out the front window, likely thinking, *Where in the heck is she going now?* I actually started laughing at the thought of the conversation going on in my living room as I squealed my tires in the road and got out of there.

Driving around the neighborhood, without any destination, I began looking closely at houses, many of which were complete fixer-uppers. I noticed that some were on the level of being condemned. I turned into one driveway with a for sale sign in the yard. I couldn't believe the house was empty.

I felt so confused. This house is nine houses down from mine, yet I had never really noticed it–let alone that it was for sale. If the kids were little, I would have known these neighbors. Now, I live like I have no neighbors. Work, home, clean, bed is now my daily routine. Then, it is work, home, clean, and bed again–so boring.

Walking around the yard, I was very interested in this brush-covered house. I found myself looking in every window, thinking about how I could make this house beautiful. I climbed right up on the cement blocks by the front window and peered into the glass.

I was soon lost in thought, planning how I could design this room or that room. I considered how a nice coat of paint would make this house come alive. I even took a few pictures with my cell phone, as if I were going to go to the bank, as if I was ready to buy this house!

Getting bored with this very expensive fantasy, I traveled back home. As I pulled into my driveway, I asked myself, out loud, "Christine, why on earth did you paint your house gray? You used to have a beautiful, soft-yellow house, with hunter green shutters." The sun faded the color out, which was not supposed to happen. Since it did happen, insurance covered the new paint job. "And, you chose gray, Christine? Isn't that like walking into Baskin-Robbins and choosing vanilla–not French vanilla or vanilla bean–just vanilla ice cream, the same as boring gray?" My head felt like it might explode. I didn't know how to shake off this mood.

My whole family was still sitting in the cluttered, half-dusted family room. Parked in their usual spots on their cell phones, they didn't even hear me blow into the house.

I hoped to awaken everyone's digital-device spell, so I announced loudly as I clapped my hands in the air, "Were moving; I am tired of working for a house. I am *totally* tired of working for *this* house!"

This, of course, sent everyone scattering like ants being sprayed with bug spray. Why? Because they all know this mood! This is the mood where I begin cleaning walk-in closets and firing off crazy, loud orders like a drill sergeant. They know that I will soon be barking out to no one in particular, "Pick up those shoes, and why is this in this room? Here, pick this up too!"

I began asking everyone in earshot unanswerable, loaded questions. You know, the questions that no one better answer or Heaven help them questions? Questions like, "Why did I paint this room in earth tones? Was I crazy that day when I thought shades of mud would make me happy? Why didn't you tell me, 'Too many browns, Mother'? You have an opinion about everything else; why did you hold your tongue about this?" Those kinds of questions left my mouth as I picked up everything in my path.

When my son reappeared in the kitchen, he looked sleepy eyed, but fresh and ready to go. "Good morning to you too, Mother," he said to me in a derogatory tone as he leaned in to give me a big bear hug. This hug automatically makes my ick with the world a thing of the past. Damn this kid! He holds magical powers over my heart; I know this for sure. It's like he can sprinkle magic dust over my head, and poof, angry is gone! Well, temporarily anyways.

"Good morning to you, my darling son, Eddie," I said as I pretended to tap an imaginary watch on my wrist. I did this because it was eleven thirty, and he had to be at work in thirty minutes. However, I already had his uniform washed and folded in the laundry room, with his belt, socks, cleaned shoes, name tag, and work hat sitting nicely in the chair waiting for him in the kitchen.

He just leaned in my direction and flashed me another huge smile. Then shrugged his shoulders and proceeded to take a huge swig out of a two liter, standing in nothing but his boxer briefs.

"Moooooom, stop stressing; I've got plenty of time." He tapped his imaginary watch on his wrist, as if to mock me. Then, I saw him shaking his head as he disappeared into another area of the house before I could start my lecture on punctuality.

My son has always been so carefree. He was the happiest baby; he was actually born with a happy, carefree air about him. Emily, she was happy, quiet, and so well behaved. That's because she would never let me out of her sight. I didn't mind, though. I was fortunate enough to stay home with them. Now, I am not saying in any way this is why he was so happy or she was so well behaved. I don't want to piss off the working mothers of the world. Trust me, I have been both. Actually, I only stayed home with them until Emily was in kindergarten. Then, it was off to work for me.

In my mind, my job was to be their mother and hopefully create happy, well-adjusted kids. Now, they are teens, alien creatures whom I don't understand sometimes. I think when you become a mother, you forget about being a teenager yourself, as if that period in your own life didn't really exist. Did it?

Quickly flashing back to my adolescence, I remember that I was horrible! I think I was plotting to run away from home from the time I came out of my mother's womb. Crazy, but so true. I always had a fascination with other places. Or, any place I wasn't at that moment. I was definitely born with wings.

Standing at the kitchen sink, staring out the window, I found myself transfixed with my back yard. It's almost as if I can shut my eyes and easily be transported to yesterday. I have so many memories in storage. I can pull them up at will, and all these images radiate from that six-second hug from my son. I let out a sad little sigh.

I can remember Eddie had the best imagination. Both of them did. I encouraged being silly. Now, silly is usually them mocking me and calling me "The Goober."

When the kids were little, I delighted in doing anything and everything to the fullest. When he was four, I painted a life-sized mural on Eddie's bedroom wall of the Teenage Mutant Ninja Turtles. He would talk to them about his day while lying in his bunk bed at night. He would hold his little Fischer Price flashlight, and he would tell each one goodnight and that they would be best friends forever.

My son became fascinated with the Turtles when they were not readily available like they are now. My friend Tony let him watch an ancient VHS of one of their movies one night at his dinner party.

Tony came out with this dusty video, without a box, smiling and saying, "Hey, buddy, I have the best movie in the whole world! It is still my favorite. Do you like ninjas?" Eddie had never heard of *ninjas*, but immediately he wanted more! After he started watching it, he came out every so often to ask us to rewind certain parts of the movie; he even learned the theme song by the end of the night.

After we got home from this dinner party, the Teenage Mutant Ninja Turtle video played all day. Even if Eddie wasn't watching it, from the other room, he was listening to it. He magically learned every line, every karate move, and every song. Now, I would have never accepted this video tape if I had known that in 1997 Turtle stuff did not exist–anywhere! It was popular in, like, 1984, and had not resurfaced yet. I had such a hard time finding anything to do with Ninja Turtles.

I gave my mother strict orders, five states away, "If you find any toy, I don't care if it's a chewed-up bath toy, please buy it!" She did; she found all kinds of stuff, including bed sheets and a vintage lunch box. But in between my mother's good fortune, I was stuck with one sad little VHS tape that was going to melt if we played it more than once a day.

I remember finding an old Ninja Turtles comic book at a garage sale. I held it up to the sky, shouting, "How much for this?" I acted like I had found the Holy Grail itself! I was willing to pay whatever the woman asked.

After we read it cover to cover, night after night, sounding out the sound effects each time, I had a light-bulb moment. I would paint Eddie a mural of the Ninja Turtles!

I went down to our library and rented a wall projector. I paid twenty-five dollars for the week and begged the librarian to please give me a few extra days for free, if I needed it. I photocopied each character onto a transparency and then blew each one up on the wall, making them life-sized. I traced it all with a number two pencil on his wall for days. Then,

I painted each one until he came to life, sometimes forcing myself to stay up until three o'clock a.m.

The day had finally come. I was finished painting them. It was an awesome mural. Each one had his weapon of choice and his name signed below. At the top of the scene, it said on a sign, "Cowabunga, Eddie!" I really could not believe how cool it looked!

Ed and I told Eddie after breakfast that some new friends dropped by to see him, and they were in his room. He said, "My room? Dad, quit joking with me!"

I had to convince him to go peek! He walked across the house. Ed and I stood in the hallway to get his reaction. I wish I could have taped it, because I am convinced, to this day, that his reaction would have won the grand prize on *America's Funniest Home Videos*.

Eddie peeked in his door, screamed at the top of his lungs, and then slammed the door shut. He started dancing and singing, reciting their names. He ran up to Ed and I, and shouted, "The Turtles are in my house! The Ninja Turtles!" He went back into his room and started introducing himself to them, carrying on a full conversation, telling them about his favorite parts in the movie.

Ed's parents would usually surface on Sundays for the traditional Italian dinner I would make–if Ed was home and off the road. They came to visit with the grandkids and tell Ed, when I left the room, what a mess things were around the house.

I can remember Eddie taking my mother-in-law by her hand, so excited, into his bedroom to meet his "best friends in the whole universe," as he referred to his Ninja Turtle mural now. Soon after, I overheard her say to Ed, "Why on earth would you let her do that to the wall? What on earth has gotten into you, Ed? That is going to be awfully hard to scrub off that wall!" That's all the woman said, and then she left the room, with not another word.

Ed didn't care; he just shrugged his shoulders and told her, "It makes Eddie very happy." Besides, he knew there was no stopping me, not when my mood hits with a creative surge. Watch out! Here I come!

That comment to his mother is something I will always treasure about Ed when I think back to when the kids were little. Plus, he once told me, as we were lighting sparklers with the kids in the driveway on a Thursday night, for no special reason, that he would probably have been a much happier person if he had a mother like me. No idea of mine was too crazy for him.

When I thought about his mother's comment, all I could think of was, *Whoa, let me?* The only way to properly describe my mother-in-law is to say she behaves exactly like the character Marie Romano from *Everybody Loves Raymond*. I am Debra, Ray's wife.

For the past twenty-some years, every single birthday card and Christmas card they give to me is signed, "From Ed's Mom and Dad." They always hand my card to Ed and tell him, "Here, give this to *her*." Twenty-three years later, I am only referred to as *she* or *her*. Good Lord, people! I gave birth to your grandkids. Smile already!

On the day of the mural comment, all I could think was, *Poor Eddie!* To this day, I remember his face and how it fell after her comment. I can also remember talking with him that night as he got into his pjs. He asked me if I was in trouble for painting those Turtles on his wall. He was leaning against the wall with his arms stretched out, as if he was hugging them.

I let him know right away that the Ninja Turtles wrote me a letter. I said, "In this letter, they each asked me, your mommy, if they could be your best friends. They explained that I could trust them *all*, to be very good friends to you." He did not miss a beat, and of course, he asked to see these letters.

I pretended to take a shower, only to come out with my same clothes on and a towel wrapped around my dry hair. I read to him, over and over, the quick letters I had written in crayon. He still remembers this, and I still have the letters.

That will always be one of the moments I think of when times get hard, and I worry if I did right for my children. Being a mother was all I ever wanted, but that desire alone doesn't ensure that I did everything correctly.

The kids and I had a lot of time just the three of us. All of my family lives in Ohio, and Ed's parents live about forty-five minutes away. Ed spent weeks driving on the road to support us. So, we were it–especially before they started school and started making friends of their own.

We camped out in tents in the back yard. We had movie parties where the house was lined with sleeping bags, where I slept in one too. One time, I even moved all the furniture out of the living room and took every spare sheet in the house and draped them from the ceiling fans, creating a circus-like tent. We couldn't go to the real thing, so I would bring the circus to them. The kids and I spent days under our circus tent. We would dance or be an animal; we did magic tricks and played hours of charades.

One summer, I covered the vaulted ceiling in the family room with glow-in-the dark stars so that we could lie under the stars on a blanket to read our favorite stories to each other. Yes, we could have gone outside, but the Florida bugs at night in the summer will eat you alive.

For weeks, we had three huge refrigerator boxes that sat in the foyer. We made and created them into cabins, complete with string phones connected to each one.

We had water day out in the yard, until every inch of grass in my side yard was muddy soup. I would chalk giant hopscotch boards on the driveway. All the neighborhood kids would stay with us, shooting hoops, ridding scooters and big wheels, or doing hopscotch in the driveway until the streetlights would come on. I took pride giving my kids parts of me I had waited my whole life to share.

We would go to the library and pick out a ton of books and read them by flashlight in my bed on a Friday night, giggling and laughing until way past bedtime. We would take nature walks with our mason jars to collect bugs. We would pack up and spend the day at the local springs or the beach.

There are so many things I miss about them being little. It seems like I had an easier time living in the moment when they were younger. How did I become such a rigid mess? Who in the hell am I now?

My brow started to sweat as I realized I am really seriously going to suffer with empty nest syndrome. I define so much of me with being their mother. Suddenly, I felt big alligator tears rolling down my cheeks. I quickly wiped them away. What? I didn't realize I was standing there crying.

I wiped out the sink and wiped countertop off, even though, surprisingly, this area of my house was truly spotless. I decided to go outside and rake some leaves. I quickly headed for the front door for fear someone would alert Ed and tell him, "Daaaad, Mom is crying!"

Then I would have to spend fifteen minutes telling him that I don't know what's up. Really, Ed.

REALLY? 8

I then found myself in the yard saying, for myself to hear, "Clear your mind, Christine. Just breathe. Don't think about a thing." I don't know about you, but when I force something on myself, it just feels so phony. I have tried yoga and meditation, only to be left feeling even more out of sorts because I could not get to that place everyone gushed about after class.

I began to think, *Maybe I am supposed to be still. Maybe I should not rake leaves, but find my inner quiet.* I decided to sit down right where I was raking and give my body a chance to relax.

I heard the birds singing away; it sounded so pretty. I heard cars behind me on the road, stopping at the stop sign fifty feet from my yard. I noticed a barking dog. *Okay, this isn't so bad,* I thought. I actually found myself starting to relax. It was a beautiful day. I could feel the soon-to-be noon sun start to peek through the enormous oak trees and warm my face. I quickly dried my wet eyelashes and runny nose.

"Mom, are the towels dry yet?" my son hollered out the front door as he stood there in his boxer briefs and nothing else.

He shouted again, "Helloooooo! Dad wants to know, just in case you're wondering!" As he closed the door, I heard him say, "I dunno what she is doing; she isn't answering me, and she is weird."

Putting my face in my hands, I tried not to laugh or cry again at how insane that just was. Like, really? You can't open the dryer and see if the towels are dry yet? Really, son?

I decided to abandon the antique rake and the sad little piles of leaves I had attempted to rake up. Struggling to stand, I rolled around on the grass and made my way to the house to see if I could salvage this mood.

"Are you taking a break? Can I get you something to drink?" my husband quickly asked me, as I blew through the house, heading straight for the bedroom.

Believe me, after all the years we have been together, I knew he had not asked my son to come and find me to ask me if the towels were dry. More likely, Ed had asked my son if the towels were dry. My son, I am betting, thought it would be much easier to ask me than to look in the damn dryer himself.

"No, I am not taking a break. I lost interest in the whole leaves thing," I said to him in an agitated tone, trying not to mention the dryer *thing*. As I sat down to my computer to download some music, Ed turned on the TV.

I heard him huffing and puffing as he went back into the kitchen. He was talking to the dog, as if she was the only one really able to understand his dilemma of the un-raked leaves. Then he started making "tut-tut" sounds with his tongue as he disappeared through the garage to go outside.

I found myself getting up from my computer and shutting the door, not even responding to his mumbling. In our house, if I shut my bedroom door, do not knock unless someone smells fire or someone is bleeding. I very rarely close my bedroom door. I actually do a horrible job in setting boundaries as a parent.

The kids will still come in my bedroom–even if I am sleeping–flip on the bathroom light, and take a shower. Note: they have their own bathroom, but tell me they "like" mine better! When Ed was gone all the time and they were little, I didn't see down the road. I didn't see the importance of rules and boundaries. I did not see today.

I cared more about other things, which are important, too, like, table manners, sharing, compassion, and forgiveness. I taught them about apologizing without being asked and how to listen to others when they speak. One thing I didn't teach was the importance of boundaries.

Truth be told, I knew why I was in a "piss-poor mood," as Grandma Rose always used to say to me. She would always follow that expression with, "Go ahead and be pissed off, because being pissed off, Chrissie, is better than being pissed on!" Lord, Grandma Rose had a wickedly funny sense of humor.

Anyway, I was in this mood because I was worried sick that when I return to work Monday morning there will be a note from the answering service waiting on the fax machine. I could see it typed in cold, harsh, black and white font: "Claudia is in Volusia County Hospice." I couldn't sleep the night before, worrying that her daughter didn't make it to her bedside on time. I did not get to say good-bye or tell her how good her pumpkin bread was.

Deciding to put off downloading music for a moment, I sunk into my bed and gave in to my television. A *Real Housewives* marathon was playing for the next six hours or so. *That should give me plenty of time to chill out,* I thought.

I laughed at myself, thinking what my opening montage would be if I was chosen to be one of the jaded housewives on the Bravo Network. I was laughing out loud, just thinking about Orange City Housewives. I decided my intro might be something like, "I am dangerously funny. I will use my fantastic humor to build you up, but also cleverly to tear you down! All in good taste, though, darling."

I picture myself twirling around and striking a pose in some bleach-splattered sweat pants with my socks and flip-flops. Well, maybe that's too much.

Reader, am I making you think, *Huh? Is she like Honey Boo Boo's mother?* The answer is no; my kids have funny nicknames, but I better change my outfit.

Re-do. Instead, I should be twirling around in an outfit I bought from the mall, with a knock-off designer bag. I would wave at the viewing audience and blow kisses. The whole time, I would be pointing at myself, like, *Look at me, Mom!*

During the commercial breaks, I found myself getting annoyed with the whole network. I was shouting at the TV, "Really Bravo? Why can't you make a show about *real* people?" I think, *Maybe I am just bitter. Who am I fooling anyway? I love this show and any of the cities that feature these women called "housewives"! What is wrong with me?*

Then, it occurred to me, *After my marathon is over, I will hunt down the executives of Bravo through cyberspace. Yeah! I will send them an email. A letter!* Finding some scratch paper, I began to write a letter, thinking, *Why should I wait?* I was feeling very happy with my creative energy. I begin firing off the letter:

Dear Mr. or Ms. Reality Television,

My life is rich, full of voyeur-esque possibility. I go to a regular nine o'clock to five o'clock job in healthcare for a meager wage. Isn't that exciting? Wait, I know! I am also dealing with growing teens, a husband of twenty years, and stacks of unpaid bills. I come home at night to find a feisty Chihuahua that has peed everywhere. Excuse me? That is nail biting, water-cooler-talk worthy! Is it not?

Correct me if I am wrong, but making a family pack of chicken breasts last for three meals *is* completely imaginative. Plus, it takes cunning skill to please these people I live with!

I can talk in a monotone voice and say, "Bible," when I want people to believe what I am saying–just like the Kardashian's. Whoops! I know it is another network, but go with it!

I would be happy to ride in my van and scream, like Vickey from Orange County, "Woo hoo, my love tank is finally full!" Or, if you want, I will strap on a donkey bootie and pretend that my husband loves an ass as big as the state of Texas, like Phaedra from Atlanta. I would go the distance and get a nose job and have an unveiling party at a local fast food restaurant, like the new and improved Kim from Orange County. I promise I could throw down some "crazy eyes" like Ramona from New York–just ask my kids. They know crazy eyes when I flash the *look* at them!

I, however, cannot promise any expensive shopping trips, being that most days my bank account sits roughly at thirty dollars positive. But, we can go shopping at Target. I could wander around the store and see what imagination and random, left-over gift cards from Christmas could buy us. That is true reality! Boring and normal will make the ratings soar!

For you, Bravo, I am willing to sacrifice. Stick your toe in the deep end! America really does want to see some "real" people on your channel.

Before I end this letter, I have a request. Could you please just let one of the cast members from *New Jersey* Housewives–I don't care which one because I love them all, but I do believe Carolyn and I would have a ton to talk about–drive Andy Cohen down to Florida to visit me? You could film it all, of course! We could even go to Miami to visit Mama Elsa!

I do solemnly swear, the ratings will be out of this world! Why? Because people are starving to see *real!* They want to see a regular girl living in a regular world–like me!

Sincerely,

Christine Marie Malone

(A closet *Housewives* fan)

P.S. Which new city you will be featuring in the fall? Just curious!

Dysfunctional 9

I t is no secret, and I will profess it to anyone: I love television, movies, theater, and Broadway plays–any of it and all of it!

I cannot really pinpoint when my fascination with television started. I just remember always loving it. One show that I could never miss an episode of was *The Wonderful World of Disney* on Sunday nights. As a kid, waiting for that music to start was unbearable. Walt, Mr. Disney himself, would be sitting there in the opening scene, eagerly waiting to reveal what we, the viewers, would see for the next hour. It was captivating.

I loved sitcoms, too–especially ones that were forbidden for kids at our house, like the television show *Soap*. I loved it. My dad would get home from work, and I would start quoting jokes Billy Crystal's character had said on the show. My dad would say, "No more *Soap*, Christine. Turn off the TV!" I would throw a fit, not realizing it really was not humor for eight-year-olds. Why? Because I got the jokes.

I believed I was truly genius, morphing into different actresses after watching a television show or movie. I can remember riding my bike around the neighborhood, sporting my Dorothy Hamill hair cut–with a giant cowlick in the back of my head, no less. I remember wishing I had a flashy, one-piece jumpsuit like the amazing girls on *Charlie's Angels*. I was jealous of the store-bought, real jumpsuits the bratty girls from down the street wore.

I had no problem improvising. I used to pull my pants way up and over my jacket and tuck my socks into my shoes. Then I would draw hearts and stars all over my hands and arms with markers for special powers. Not for one minute did I think I looked insane.

As I think back, I feel bad for my little sister. As we zoomed around the neighborhood on our bikes, she usually peddled furiously behind me trying to keep up. She was often whining, "Please stop calling me Charlie!"

You see, both my dad and my brother have the name Charlie. Poor kid, knowing me, I probably never explained to her that she was my Charlie from *Charlie's Angels*. I always used to say to her, "Rodger that, Charlie!" Then I would take off, riding all over, looking for the other angels. I think I missed my mark with acting.

Let's see. What else did I like to watch? *Laverne and Shirley* made me realize girls were just as cool as boys; you could work in a factory and drink beer. *The Muppets* let me see really cool musicians and actors being silly and funny with puppets. *The Love Boat* and *Fantasy Island* showed me you have to be smart in a man's world. *General Hospital* taught me how to make out. *The Facts of Life* taught me that other people had bongs in their house, too! Carol Burnett and Tim Conway taught me how to get people to laugh.

Since I have trotted down memory lane, being all nostalgic with TV, I just realized something. Marion on *Happy Days* was a cougar, way before her time! The Fonz absolutely loved her. Go, Marion! Hysterical!

Grandma D loved movies on television; she was my dad's mom. She helped pave the way for my love of black and white movies–or any movie with Marilyn Monroe, Judy Garland, Clark Gable, Andy Rooney, Barbara Streisand, Tony Curtis, Elizabeth Taylor, Humphrey Bogart, Grace Kelly, or Jimmy Stewart. Oh, I could go on for days. These are just a few of the great actors who flood my memory when I think of her.

Grandma D was classy, old-school Hollywood glamour. She even smoked her cigarettes in those long black extenders, just like the beautiful women I studied in these films. She would blow mystical smoke rings in the air and then pull little pieces of left-over tobacco off her tongue, never messing up her perfect red lips. And she could do all of this while she talked on her pink telephone that was the size of a loaf of bread.

Every inch of her makeup was spectacular, as were her clothes and accessories. Everything was polished, pressed, and color-coordinated. Her carefully calculated bleach blond updo was sprayed down with more hair spray than anyone one person should breathe in a lifetime. If she had stood under a helicopter, it would have still looked flawless.

She and I used to watch hours of television, when my siblings and I were dropped off at her house. When my parents left, I had no idea where they went, nor did I care. I just wanted to know when they would be home, exactly. Grandma D would have all the best programs underlined in her TV guide, and we would be ready for our day. I needed to calculate my time to figure out what shows I could watch until they returned.

At my house, kids did not sit around and watch television. It was usually turned off during the day, especially when we were little, and always on the weekends. We were told, "Outside! Go play!" Heck, my sister and brothers knew I would play if we all played TV tag. Before someone tags you, you have to scream out a television show. If you didn't get your words out in time, you were tagged "it."

I could always name a show, which frustrated them to no end! However, if I wasn't riding my bike, you could usually find me lying around in the front yard sulking, thinking about what I was probably missing on TV. Maybe I was a really weird kid and didn't realize it.

Life was so hard in middle school, being the chubby, poor kid. It was unbearable at times. There were no anti-bullying campaigns in the 80's. Television helped me forget about a lot. Even if I couldn't totally forget, it definitely kept my superior imagination very active.

I guess if I am like any one TV character that is in the present, or I should say, if I identify with any one character, it would be someone like

Liz Lemon from *30Rock*. Really, I get her weirdness and her constant quest to find the answers. I relate to the girl who feels forever misunderstood. Plus, she is witty and funny. And, there is one other key point: hello, it's Tina Fey! She, to me, is the word *priceless*.

On the other hand, I am totally Cam from *Modern Family*. Really, I am that gay character. Sound impossible? Wrong. Every time I watch that show, I giggle in delight. Even my kids say, "Wow! Are you sure the writers of this show don't know you?" Cam's flare, his theatrics, his drama–I love every piece of it.

There are only four men I have ever surrendered my heart to. Besides my dad, my husband, and my son, there is Daren. There aren't really any memories from my childhood that do not include him. It is so hard to accept sometimes that life has driven a wedge between us. We don't see much of each other these days. Once upon a time, I couldn't go six hours without talking to Daren.

I first met Daren while riding my bike down the street in front of my childhood home. I stopped on the sidewalk that day. I guess I had no choice; the chain on my bike had broken. So, I stopped.

There I sat on the sidewalk, eating my penny candy. I had actually bought an impressive amount from collecting couch-cushion change. It was 1979. Daren rode up on his metallic green bicycle, with a metallic purple banana seat. He was wearing these hysterical short shorts with a bright yellow sweater. Lord, we were two misfits destined to meet.

He just parked his bike and came up and sat down with me. We started talking to each other on that sidewalk and stayed for over an hour. We didn't even introduce ourselves until the street lights came on, signaling to both of us to go home. It was as if we had known each other forever. It was kismet between us from that very first hello.

We fell in and out of love with each other our whole childhood. He was my first everything–except sex. He was even my first sleep over; my parents were very liberal hippies. They didn't care if a boy was sleeping over. Plus, my mom told me years later she always knew Daren was gay, and she was fine with it. Even though the town I grew up in was a very sheltered Midwest town, my parents were not prejudiced about anything or anyone. They never taught us being gay was wrong. Even though my childhood was filled with a lot of things I want to erase, I know the gift of accepting others the way they are is the best gift my parents ever gave me.

Daren never said a word to me about his orientation, even though he said he knew in the second grade he was gay. He wanted to wait until he was far, far away from his father before coming out. Daren was my first date at a school dance and my first friend to be dropped off at the movies together. We went to our first concert together. We started every grade together, from the third grade through our senior year. We shared a locker in high school; we taught each other how to drive and drank our first sip of alcohol together. We took our first road trip together.

Before we did anything with anyone else, we always checked in with each other first–not because we had to, but because we wanted to. We never referred to each other as boyfriend or girlfriend. In our eyes, we were just friends. I did find out, though, that in my sophomore year he had told guys he was my boyfriend so they would leave me alone. That led to a very explosive, argumentative summer between us, but we got through it.

I would come home from a date, and he would be hanging out in my room. My parents? Trust me; they did not care. They were too busy entertaining their own friends to even know what my brothers, sister, and I were up to. We would lie in my bed until dawn, listening to music and planning our futures–futures filled with amazing adventure. We both had the most dysfunctional families in the entire town, so that helped bond us instantly.

One year, I dressed up as a librarian for Halloween. Yes, yes, I did. My costume was complete with a little blue blazer, bun in my hair, and even the tortoise-shell glasses. I ended up throwing all my candy in the street that I had collected from a long night of trick-or-treating. Why? Because everyone thought my costume was hysterical. In my world, it was not a joke! To me, that was the coolest job in the world. Spend all day with books? Sign me up!

That Halloween stung, and the experience wounded my heart. The night ended with my mother telling me, "Christine! I should have drowned you in the bathtub when I had the chance! All those stretch marks for *you*?" My tears fell in confusion. How could no one understand my costume? My disappointment and emotion were messy details my mother could not or would not tolerate after an entire day of drinking. For many years, I usually went to sleep wondering how she could say such awful things to me.

That is, until I met Daren. He understood my costume. He stayed with me that night, reading to me by flashlight, sharing even his best candy with me. I just knew deep down that Daren would never hurt me, not mentally, physically, or sexually. I never built up any walls with him; we loved each other unconditionally.

Sitting in my grown-up bedroom on that moody Saturday, I realized that if anyone knows how to snap me out of a *mood*, it's Daren! Forgetting that he may try to force Peach Schnapps down my throat to relax me, I grabbed my phone and hit dial.

"Hey, it's me. What are you up to today?" I asked, before he had time to tell me he was busy.

"Well, well. If it isn't my friend. What is your name again? Oh, it's the girl who is always too busy for me," he said to me, and then he paused and started talking to someone in the background.

"Me? What? It's you, my friend, who is always too busy!" I said, laughing, knowing that this was a losing argument. I bailed on his housewarming party a couple of months ago, and I am worried he is still going to be pissed with me still.

"Well, I am in the middle of entertaining thousands of tourist from all over the Midwest-no, make that the world. Why? What did you have in mind?" he asked in a suspicious tone, and then I heard him set the phone down to answer another call.

"Okay, so what do you have in mind?" he asked me, as I heard a cash register ringing in the background.

He works for The Mouse. He has worked there for over twenty years. We moved to Florida together in 1990 to work at Disney. We were young, dumb, and broke. However, the thrill of moving to Florida only made sense if we did it together.

"Well, are you interested in some shoe therapy?" I asked him, giggling, knowing shoes are a serious weakness for him.

"Why? Why do you do this to me? You know damn well that it makes me sick to say no to shoes! Andi, what else? I am broke until payday." He sighed a much-exaggerated sigh, and then he asked me to wait a few minutes. He had to walk across the park and over to security to file a claim. Being on his cell phone while walking through the magical park is not allowed, ever!

I hollered in the receiver, "SHOES!" I knew he put his phone in his shirt pocket, and I heard him shout back, even though it was a little muffled, "Stop it, Andi!" I lay back on my bed, waiting for him to come back to me.

He has called me Andi since we were fifteen. Why? Because that's the year the movie *Pretty in Pink* came out. The main character in the movie is named Andi. Daren was convinced someone must have followed us around and written that script based off our relationship.

Yes, I was that poor girl who loved to sew and make really cool clothes. I was dating rich guys from private schools, who were way out of my league. Daren was Ducky, Andi's lovable but annoying best friend. In our Spanish class that year, the teacher asked me what Spanish name I wanted? Daren answered for me; he said, "Andi," after this character. So, for thirty years, to Daren, I am Andi.

"Are you there? Is everything okay? I am sitting in a backstage lot; you have ten minutes." Waiting for me to respond, he says, "Nine minutes, Andi! I mean it; I don't want to be seen here sitting with my phone." He said not another word.

"I think I am having a midlife crisis. I am sorry I missed your housewarming party. Please, don't be pissed at me. Please. Ed was on the road, and you know how I am about showing up at parties by myself." I paused to take another deep breath to finish.

"My kids are growing up, and they don't need me anymore. It's heartbreaking. All they ever ask for are dry towels and money. I am worried that my patient will die this weekend, and I won't get to say goodbye. My skinny pants were too tight today, and I hate that I painted my house gray. I hate that my best friend lives forty-five minutes away. And, I feel old. I am having a case of the 'I miss the Andi and Daren days.' Don't you miss us?" I said, feeling very winded, as if I just dialed 1-800 dial a shrink.

Waiting for his response, I reached in my nightstand and started unwrapping a handful of chocolate kisses, putting them in my mouth two at a time.

"Are you eating? I hear wrappers and chewing. Do you want your fat pants to be too tight?" He started laughing at his therapy, repeating the words *fat pants* a couple of times as if it was the funniest thing he had heard all day.

"Yes, I am eating chocolate, loads of it. I have teens in the house, so no wine cellar or booze at this address. Do you know why? I worry every night when I go to bed they will be like you and me, stealing every ounce of the alcohol in the house while their parents are sleeping!" I quickly shoved three more rounds of chocolate in my mouth, exaggerating my chewing in the phone so he could hear every bite.

"Oh, boo-hoo. You know your kids will never be as bad as their mother was! I haven't heard you like this in a while. Is Ed home? Will he be okay if we go out? You know he likes to keep you on a tight leash," he said this in a very matter-of-fact tone. He knew it was not true, but he was trying to get a rise out of me.

"Shoes, lots of shoes, Daren. I am going to buy them without you." I twisted the shoe knife a little deeper into his side for making a comment like that.

"All your chocolate chewing is making me hungry. Can you put Sensa on chocolate?" He asked me as we hear a beep on his phone, signaling to us both he has another call. He answered it without even telling me to hold on.

Waiting in the silence, his phone started playing Pat Benatar's "We Belong." I thought to myself, *How odd; why this song? Only Daren would have music playing while he keeps his caller waiting. Is this an app I don't know about yet?*

I remember he made a mix tape of all Pat Benatar's songs for me to listen to on the way home from New Jersey. We listened to it for seventeen hours on the car ride home. I had called him in a panic to come and get me, to rescue me. With no questions asked, he came.

After high school, the fall after we graduated actually, I moved to New Jersey and became a nanny for a family with three kids. Everyone I knew was going off to college or traveling to Europe or moving somewhere cool. Everyone except me. Even Daren was going to college.

My job at the local hotel certainly wasn't going to get me to Europe- not on my wages. By the time I figured out I needed to get my crap together as a student, it was too late. Plus, my plan was to live in NYC someday. In my mind, way before the creation of *Sex in the City*, I wanted to be Carrie Bradshaw. Making it on my own in New York City and moving as far away from the backwards, dated town where I grew up was all I ever thought about. If being a nanny in New Jersey was a way to get me closer to my dream, then so be it.

I graduated high school as an average student. I could have been the best student that high school had ever seen. My teachers saw it. I surprised them all, all the time. I even surprised myself sometimes.

Mr. Steele, my English teacher, started the last half of our senior year introducing us to Shakespeare's *Romeo and Juliet*. I had already read it from cover to cover many times. But, I sat and listened, trying not to let my mind wander. Deciding to drift anyways, I started thinking how I too had just suffered a heart break.

My boyfriend of five months had decided to give me the speech. You know, the "it's me, not you" speech. He told me he wanted me to experience my senior year being free, not tied down. He said that we owed it to each other to date other people before we graduated. It didn't dawn on me there was already someone else in his life until I handed him his class ring and got out of his car. I just stood under the streetlight at the end of my driveway in the frosty midnight air, crying and feeling so stupid. Even then, I was wishing Daren was at my door.

Snapping out of my daydream and clearing my mind of my break-up trance, I came back to class. Mr. Steele asked what the major difference was between the characters in the story and the teens today.

Everyone was saying things like clothes and the way they spoke or that there was no electricity or running water and no automobiles in Romeo's time. Yawn. Most days I could not believe I had to breath the same air as these idiots.

Keep in mind, as outgoing as I am now, once upon a time, I was a very shy girl. Teachers usually saw that as being lazy. What most teachers didn't realize was that I was terrified to speak. Besides, I was raised in a home where kids were told on an hourly basis sometimes that kids should been seen, not heard.

Plus, teachers and students were always comparing me to my infamous, very popular, older brother. This was something I could never shake off in my high school days.

Mr. Steele said, "How about you, Christine? Do you have anything to add?" Never once did he suspect such an answer would come from my mouth. I don't think I had spoken out loud the entire year until that day.

"There are no differences, if you think about it. This was written how long ago? Love is still just as brilliant, spectacular, and magical. A broken heart can leave you feeling like you can't breathe, live, or go on. The pure, utter pain of broken love can hurt so much. When you are in love, you don't see "things." You only see the beauty in love. As far as I can tell, the only difference is the calendar years that have passed since that story was written. Love transcends through time. People will read that story a thousand years from now and understand it, connect with it, and believe the love between the two of them," I said, as I doodled my now ex-boyfriend's name all over my notebook, trying my very best not to start bawling from my own fresh heartbreak.

He started clapping. At first, I thought he was being sarcastic, mocking me. But he went over to his desk, wrote A+ on a piece of paper, and handed it to me. He asked me to stay after class, and he gave me a book he wanted me to read.

It became a regular thing. Every week was marked by a new book. Then on Friday, he would ask me to stay after class and talk with him about it. I thought, cool, a teacher who actually thinks I am smart! I went along with it, even though I was an avid reader and had already read almost every book he gave me. But, this teacher was so popular with all students and the faculty that it was kind of a boost to my popularity status.

One word describes me, well make that two: gullible fool.

Mr. Steele turned out to be a real scumbag. The summer after I graduated, I went to a senior party, and he showed up completely drunk. He cornered me in the kitchen and proceeded to tell me how hot I was. He told me how happy he was that I was no longer his student. He had been counting down the days, he said, for the moment to tell me all this. He started every sentence by calling me "babe." Slurring his words, he kept telling me he was only fifteen years older than me. He asked if I liked older guys.

He was whispering, standing way too close, and making me so uncomfortable. As he sprayed his alcohol breath in my face, he asked me if I knew what I *did* to him. He was sure we could be so hot together, and he asked me to think about what he was saying to me. Pulling my hands towards him, he begged me to go out in the driveway and sit in his car with him so that he could tell me more about books and *other* things on his mind.

As he slid his hand up my thigh and put his drunken mouth on my neck, making my sunburn sting, Daren appeared behind him. He motioned to me from behind Steele's back to be quiet, putting his index finger up to his lips. Then Daren winked at me, signaling it would be okay.

Very slowly from behind, Daren leaned into Mr. Steele's ear. Barely audible enough for all three us to hear, he said, "Tell me, Dave, how is Monica these days?" Monica was Steele's wife, and he let some of his students call him by his first name.

As quick as lightning, Daren pulled Steele's wallet out of his back pocket. Steele froze inches from my body, not moving a muscle; he turned only his head to see who was standing behind him. He immediately started laughing when he saw it was Daren standing there, and said, "Daren, go home; your mommy is looking for you." Then he turned back to me and licked his lips. I was now squirming under his tight grip, wanting to get the hell away from him.

Daren did not go; instead, he tapped Dave on the shoulder again, leaning in even closer than before and said, "Hey, Dave, I would like you to tell me if you like this story." Again Daren gave me a sideways smile and winked at me. We spoke a nonverbal language only the two of us understood.

Steele gave Daren a half turn, still keeping one hand tight on my waist, while the other hand held his beer. "This better be good, kid," he sneered at Daren.

Daren puffed out his chest and raised all five feet, seven inches of himself. Daren seemed well over six feet tall at that moment. With eyes brimming with rage, he cleared his throat, held up his imaginary letter, and began reading.

"Hey, babe, I thought I would mail you back your wallet, since I will be out of town for a couple of weeks. We don't want Monica to find out about our hot, hot night. God, you are so awesome in bed! Plus, you were so right about older guys! Love ya, babe. P.S. Keep the bed warm. I will be home before you know it!" Daren looked at Dave with a sneering grin and then winked at me.

We all just stood there in complete silence. Steele quickly checked his back pockets, not even realizing, until then, that Daren had swiped his wallet.

Releasing his grip on me, Dave shoved me against the kitchen counter. After he was done flipping us both off with his middle finger, he turned and left.

I flung myself into Daren's arms and whispered into his ear, while I squeezed him so tightly, "And the Oscar goes to my best friend! I love you, Daren." Then I started crying, wondering, what in the hell did I do to deserve that?

Mr. Steele never got his wallet back; he didn't even ask for it. We actually took the cash out of it that night, before we threw it over the bridge that connected our town to the neighboring town. We went shoe shopping the next day with that money. Whereupon Daren proceeded to lecture me the entire day on wising up and not being so innocent with guys anymore. He said he would not be around to protect me forever. I remember laughing, thinking to myself, *Well, that's just crazy. Of course he will.* I did not listen to a word he was saying to me.

A couple of days later, I told my cousin Tami what happened that night. She lived next door to the jerk and occasionally babysat for him and his wife. She said after that incident she would see Steele running down to his mailbox, waiting in the street for the mailman to show up, even hollering to his wife from their driveway, "I will get the mail, Monica!" Serves him right, that stupid jerk. I was thinking to myself, *I hope the innocent girls that come after me have their own Daren.*

I heard Daren calling my name over the receiver, "Andi?" I realized he had me on hold for more than fifteen minutes! I thought, *Thank goodness he came back on the line. That was enough of a visit down memory lane for now!*

"Andi, hey sweetie, are you still there? I can't do anything tonight. Larry's mom is coming to dinner. If it's okay with you, I can drive up, and we can do a girls' night out tomorrow night in your area. Does this sound okay with you?" he said very sweetly–almost too sweetly.

"Of course! You know you don't even need to ask," I shot back at him in a somewhat snotty tone, quickly realizing he obliviously was not alone.

"I got it. You aren't alone. Just say yes if six o'clock is good, and you will be at my doorstep by seven. "

"Yes!" and he hung up. All I could think to myself was, *Thank you, Lord. I feel so much better.*

Heading off to the bathroom to clean up, I turned on the radio and prepared everything for my shower. I thought, *I know! I will make an Italian feast for dinner tonight. That will make everyone happy, especially Ed. I will need some brownie points stored up if Daren is coming for a night out.*

Ed is convinced Daren only surfaces in my life if he thinks I need some sort of rescuing. This causes really big tension between them and leaves me in the middle.

I told myself, *Christine, you must stop the worry train you constantly ride! It's another long hike up my Kilimanjaro.*

Red Flag–Beware! 10

Feeling better after my shower and fresh makeup, I entered my bedroom with a hopeful new attitude. Sitting down on the floor of my walk in closet, I began sifting through my jewelry box. I was humming leftover songs that were still floating through my head from my bubbly shower concert just minutes ago. I was happy that music was playing through my mind and not even once did I think about the words. I was singing "Walking on Broken Glass" by Annie Lennox.

I just love that woman. I am actually fascinated by her stoic beauty and her love of words. Her music is so powerful. Every time I turn on some Annie, I feel empowered. I now find myself looking into the mirror that hangs on the wall, posing, and turning my head in different freeze frames, as if someone was photographing me. I was trying to convince my mind, *Oh, yeah, you still got it!* I was making my best Annie face.

"Oh, yea… I am woman, uh huh, walking on broken glass, broken glass," I sat singing away at the top of my lungs, looking directly in the mirror and holding my hairbrush as a microphone.

I quickly snapped out of my concert for one and fell silent, leaning into the mirror, talking directly at my own reflection, "Annie, do you even know how fantastic you are?" I paused like, she was going to respond. I was wondering if she and Carly Simon are friends.

Next, I began singing "You're So Vain" and thought, *Now, those are two women in the music world I would give anything to hug or even sit next to. Heck, I would even just stand there and hold their purses to just to be in their presence.* The whole thought of even possibly meeting them someday left me feeling giddy and beyond happy. I made a note to self: *put it on your vision board.*

I found the perfect earrings, tucked away in a forgotten spot in my overstuffed jewelry box. I sighed as I looked around my enormous closet. A horrified queasiness washed over me. *What if someone, other than my family, could peek into the pocket door and behold all this packed-up junk?*

Well, I shouldn't have called it junk. Most of the boxes contain some sort of memory: a photo album, ancient toy, or outfits my kids wore when they were babies. Flashing back to an episode of *Hoarders*, I laughed. Isn't that what every hoarder says as her loved ones drag all her belongings out to the front yard? "It's not junk!"

"Oh, well," I said to myself. I knew my brain could not handle any more worry today.

Seeing my husband standing at his dresser, I decided to ask him if he purchased a t-shirt in the lobby, since all proceeds will go to my children's house in Africa.

He turned to me and smiled. I knew he would be the only person on this planet to understand what I had just said. He is used to my creative, but broken and fragmented, way of speaking.

"Yes, you mean your high-pitched shower concert, when you sang the same verse over and over again is t-shirt worthy? Maybe I will put one on backorder." He flashed me another huge smile as he went through an enormous stack of mail.

He used to get so upset with me that I never opened the mail. In fact, I usually left it all in the mailbox for days, until the postman would leave us a note, telling us to check our mail. Once in a while, I will send the kids down to get the mail. But, I have this thing about hating to get the mail. I don't know where it comes from or what suppressed memory I have about mail. I don't care about it; that's what it boils down too, really.

This apathy used to drive Ed to distraction. I know when the bills are due, and no one sends handwritten letters anymore-or even a card. So, what's in the mail? Nothing. I tried to understand where he was coming from. But, to me, it is another chore to add to the long laundry list that already exists for me when he is gone.

Other chores, like cutting the grass, don't bother me. Well, this is, before I had a teenage son. But when they were little, I would mow the grass, rake leaves, and fix things around the house. Plus, I did all the shopping, cleaning, parenting, homework, and bill paying. Well, you get the point, *all of it*. But the mail was something that I was not interested in or worried about.

I sound bitter. I am not–even though it does kind of sound like I am trying to convince even myself. *Like, really, no bitterness here. Right, Christine?* This is just one of the many mountains I have climbed in my life, and it's been a tough climb. I've had to learn that I can be loved without needing to do it all; I've had to learn to ask for help and that people will help–or at least my husband will.

I learned what I saw growing up. I watched my mother slave over my father my entire childhood; she did everything. We use to call her "Geisha Becky" as kids. I unwittingly continued the cycle that I was taught. Taking care of my man meant taking care of it all–as if it was a torch she passed to me. However, she eventually woke up, got sober, and became the embodiment of "I am woman; hear me roar." She earned her masters degree at the age of 50.

It makes me proud that my kids don't know the mother I grew up with. It is hard, though, to share any of my childhood memories with them. They look at me like a liar when I share, oh, for example, that one time Grandma was three sheets to the wind in the grocery store and abruptly stopped pushing the shopping cart to take off her bra in the middle of the store. As she screamed, she let everyone in a five-mile radius know that she was having a "power surge, a flipping hot flash!" All they know now is Grandma the activist, the women's rights leader, the living proof that Alcoholic Anonymous does truly keep you sober.

What I didn't realize was that I would eventually snap trying to be the martyr. And I certainly wouldn't have guessed it would be about the mail. I thought maybe one of Ed's *many* guy trips to the Bahamas or long weekends in Vegas, again with the guys, would have pushed me over the edge. But the mail? I even surprised myself with that melt down.

I didn't realize that eventually I would want to burn my superhero mother and wife cape. I didn't think that I would want to throw it into the fire pit in the backyard, pour lighter fluid on it, and maybe even say every cuss word I could think of as I watched it burn.

Often, we would pull in the driveway from picking him up from his eighteen-wheeler, and he would start in on me by saying, "Look at all those sticks in the yard! How long have the garbage cans been out at the road? How much money is in the bank?" He would overlook my freshly planted flowers as he shook his head at me.

I used to cut him some slack. Number one, his mother is crazy, and she lives in a museum. I always felt bad that Ed had to be loved by such an ice statue. She produced extremely anal kids who did not dare make a mess. Ever! Number two, he missed a lot–a whole lot–of the kids' growing up.

So, when he would get home from the road, I would usually make excuses for him instead of saying, "Really? You notice six little sticks, but not that I just trimmed the bushes? You are overlooking that I repainted the shutters! You are forgetting that I have been doing everything all by myself for two weeks while you have been gone! Nothing kind to say? Really, nothing?" Instead, I would usually go in the house and leave him in the yard to fuss with whatever was bothering him. Except on this day.

He said to me, from the end of the driveway, while sticking his hand in the mailbox, "Chris, what the hell? You aren't that busy! Why can't you ever get the damn mail? This is ridiculous, and you've got to start being more responsible." He shook his head in fatherly disappointment.

I felt like a crazed bull, and he was my mail matador. He waved the mail at me from the end of my driveway, and I didn't even think about what came next. There was no premeditation here.

I started hurling and lobbing every stick I could find laying in the front yard. He shouted, "Stop!" and tried to duck or dodge the flying wood. But I was seething, white-hot mad.

"What the heck has gotten into you?" he shouted, now covering his head with both arms and covering his precious mail. His look of surprise was more of a look of worry.

When I ran out of sticks, I dug up the earth with my bare hands and started flinging clumps of dirt at him. I even took out my anger on the poor bushes! I pulled leaves off the bushes! Catching my breath as I paced around the yard in tiny circles, I put my hands on my hips, digging the balls of my feet into the freshly cut grass. I stared right back at him, as if the mail, still in his hands, was a red flag! My red flag!

He stood in silent shock. Not giving up, I had new energy after my twenty seconds of pacing and started firing more random pieces of nature at him.

I ran up to him, forced the mail out of his ironclad grip, and ripped it into tiny shreds as he stood there, now with his mouth gapping open. I threw it all over the lawn, as if a piñata had exploded everywhere. I did this with relish, while laughing like a lunatic.

Then, I proceeded to scream every random thing I had done for him and the kids for the past ten years. This was an enormous list, for which I never once heard thank you–ever! I continued stomping around the yard, tearing the already torn mail into even smaller pieces.

Ending my rampage, I decided to ask him if he really thought I enjoyed washing his shit stains out of his underwear. I screamed, "Guess what, Ed? I hate it! Do you know why you don't know this? Because you are so damn busy telling me what a shitty job I do when you were gone!" I swear we looked like lunatics or something that might take place at one of my mother's hillbilly family reunions in southern Ohio.

I was so pumped up with adrenaline that I could have reshingled the roof right then. But, what goes up must come down, right? He spent the next half an hour picking up all the confetti-torn mail, while I sat watching TV.

I tried to tell myself I didn't care, but thoughts of my rampage aggravated me as I sat and cried. I knew I was better than that. My crazy performance on the front lawn had people dragging their dogs by their leashes to get away from a possible injury, to stay clear of whatever I was throwing at my husband.

I just sat and sobbed until he came in the house. I explained to him, through gagging, pitiful sobs as he rubbed my back, "I just don't want us to be like our parents, but we are turning into them!"

We have since learned how to communicate. Well, sort of. The problem with the two of us is that we are too much alike. False assumptions come easily to us. Plus, we learned together, as we grew up, that neither of us are mind readers and that our perceptions about almost everything are different. Yes, our intuitive insight was usually on target with each other, but every once in a while, every marriage needs a reality check.

Back from my flashback, I joined him at his dresser as he was still sorting the week's mail. "Did you win the Publishers Clearing House Sweepstakes yet, my gorgeous hunk of a mailman?" I asked him as I danced around behind him, hoping to get him to laugh with me. I hoped to distract him from his mail call.

"Really? Hunk, huh? I thought mail made you physically ill," he said, grabbing me by the waist and kissing my favorite kissable place on my cheek.

"Well, yes, the mail does make me go 'postal' (ha ha); however, you would be the only mailman on this entire earth I would ever find hunky. Do you want to go to the grocery store with me?" I asked him, pulling back from his embrace to wink at him.

"No, no thank you. But, if you would like company, I will go. What are you going to get?" he asked with his head cocked to the side. I know he is thinking, *She* just *went grocery shopping.*

I immediately started grinning; he knows me so well. Maybe it's a facial expression I give him? I must look like the cat who ate the canary.

He stood and waited. Ah-ha! I realized I was twirling a piece of my hair! *Note to self: stop twirling hair; it's a dead giveaway!*

"Well, I am making Italian, your favorite. I'll do meatballs from scratch, some eggplant, uhhh, maybe some red wine. Sound good?" Damn, I realized the entire time I said that sentence, I was twirling my hair again! I quickly shoved my hand in my pocket.

"Did you dent the van again?" he asked, finally putting his mail down.

"Nope. Are you trying to imply I don't cook nice, big, thoughtful, made-with-love meals for you anymore? Why, Ed, am I that transparent?" Now, sheepishly grinning, I realized I had set myself up.

"Sounds wonderful! Are you going to make garlic rolls and maybe some tiramisu, too?" he asked, fully grinning. He was playing me, stacking the deck. He knew I was up to something. So I toyed with him a little bit.

"Sure! I guess that would be possible. But, I don't know, all those carbs usually put you right to sleep, into a food coma. You know how I get *in the mood* after a couple glasses of red wine." I smiled back, waiting to see if he would draw his next card.

"Not tonight. No food coma. Who is coming over?" he asked moving closer to me. He is so damn good.

"Oh, you know, maybe one of Eddie's friends and possibly Daren tomorrow night." I ended my sentence by closing my eyes.

"No problem. I don't mind. As long as you don't drive to wherever he drags you. And, you drink one glass of wine tonight. Food puts me in a coma; wine puts you into a double coma. Deal?" he asked, softly kissing my cheek again before swatting me on my bum and leaving the room.

Going after him, I wanted to remind him that Eddie is going to Daytona for an after party for prom. "Hey, Ed, could you please check Eddie's water in his radiator and his front tire? It has been looking flat."

"I love when you talk like a mechanic; nothing is sexier than a girl mechanic. Why, where is he going?" He was folding his arms, staring out the back door. I know he worries so much about Eddie. I do, too, but our different upbringings make us parent slightly different. Somehow, we always meet in the middle. We really listen to each other when the kids are concerned.

In fact, our upbringings were worlds apart. I know for a fact his parents did not let him have a keg party for his seventeenth birthday. I joke with Eddie from time to time, telling him we did all our training with him so that can be excellent parents to his sister Emily. I like to say this after he tells us how much we suck and don't know anything.

"Take a deep breath, okay? Daytona, after the prom. He is taking his truck." I realized I was folding my arms just like him.

"Has he given you a lot of grief this week?" He unfolded his arms and walked over to me. I knew what Ed was doing; he was trying to read me. I have never been able to lie to Ed. For instance, I twirl my hair and my voice usually goes about five octaves higher when I am trying to convince him of something.

"Well, you know. He gave me normal grief, but nothing I couldn't take care of." I was wishing Eddie would have not had a girlfriend still in high school. He wasn't going to prom, just the stuff afterwards, which I know is ten times worse then the actual dance. But, sooner or later, we are going to have to cut the apron strings, or he will be living with us forever.

"Yeah, I guess. Have you given him the lecture that cops, if you get into trouble, don't bring you home anymore?" He is worried, because on several occasions, he told Eddie some of the stuff he did as a kid, but his stories always ended with, "But the cops brought me home."

"Of course! And I gave him the drinking and driving lecture and the sex talk–until he told me to stop or his ears would bleed real blood." I was laughing at how I probably did go a little over board on the sex part with him, but I need my very handsome son to understand the rules: hands to yourself and NO means NO!

"Okay, looking forward to your dinner. What time do you think you will be home?" he asked with a sideways grin.

"Give me an hour at the store, and we can have dinner by seven?" I said, knowing in my mind that dinner would be at eight, unless I bought some tiramisu and put it one of my bowls.

BROKEN 11

Leaving Ed to enjoy his mail in peace, I drove off to the store, thinking back to when I was eighteen. I was light years away in real life experience compared to my son. Hell, when I was his age, I was boarding a plane, headed for JFK to meet the family I would be a nanny for.

I think that I accepted the job because my plane was landing in NYC. Even though they were picking me up and taking me back to Jersey, I didn't care. To step foot off that plane, retrieve my bags, and find my way to the exit of the airport would be pure Heaven.

To stand in the New York air and hear the hustle and bustle of the city and feel the grit on my face–it was all I could think about. The real perk to my job was that on the weekends I could come and go; I could explore the city! I studied my AAA maps for weeks before I left Ohio. I knew how to ride the subway before I ever stepped foot in New York City.

On the plane that day, I flew from Toledo to Detroit to NYC. En route, I saw the most beautiful man I had ever seen. He was dark, foreign, and mysterious, with beautiful jet-black hair. He was also wearing a long, caramel-color cashmere coat, and he had a stunning Rolex watch on.

There I was, Pollyanna, straight from the sticks. Well, that's how I felt about my appearance anyways. I decided that very minute, as I stared at his impeccable beauty, that I would become a cosmopolitan woman as soon as I could shop in the city.

He sat across from me in the little chairs in the airport lounge. He set his briefcase in the chair next to him, took out some papers and a pen, and started working. I put my sunglasses on, thinking it would be okay because I was going to New York. Nobody questioned a New Yorker; maybe they would think I was eccentric. Who was I kidding? I wanted to just sit and stare at him without him noticing.

As we boarded the plane, he sat in the row in front of me, diagonal from me. Every once in a while, when he would lean forward, I would catch a glimpse of his profile. I was so green! I don't know why this stranger fascinated me. When we landed, and we all got off the plane, I saw him disappear into the crowd. I thought, *Now he's probably going to go and meet his equally beautiful wife.*

Well, my plan was squashed. The family I would be a nanny for was waiting for me at the gate. They recognized me by the picture I sent the agency. I talked to so many different families. Most families wanted a Midwestern girl. That was me. I picked this family because the mom and the dad worked in the city. They had three kids: two girls and a boy. Plus, they were paying me five hundred dollars a week. I could definitely live with that. This was 1988, and there was no way could I make that back home–unless I did something illegal.

They, however, forgot to mention that their kids were absolutely horrible. Their son used to hold his breath until he passed out, which usually made the older sister run and call her mother, telling her, "She made Tippy pass out again!" That was his horrible nickname! I actually went from one dysfunctional residence to another.

Plus, they also forgot to tell me that I would be the chauffeur for the kids, driving them to and from school and the dozens of activities they were signed up for. I was to be the maid, change linens, scrub her walk in shower, clean the oven, clean all their pets' cages out, and do all the cooking and meal clean up.

She never had time to lift a finger. But, she sure did have time to make plenty of lists for me. They also left out that the two of them fought like rabid dogs, and they were sleeping in separate bedrooms.

I gave it my best. New York City was always in the back of my mind. Saturday morning would come, and I was out the door at seven am. I used to walk to the bus stop, which took me to the train station, which would take me to the Port Authority, and from there, I would get on the subway and go all over the city. By myself!

I have the most unforgettable memories from my days in the city. Going to the museums or just sitting in Times Square and watching the people thrilled me. However, finding my way to The New York Public Library was probably the single best memory I have of the city.

Well, wait. Riding the elevator up into the Twin Towers to have lunch was pretty awesome, too. I even caught a glimpse of Paul McCartney getting into a limo on the side of the street. Every Saturday, I would go back to that same spot, at the same time, to see if I might see Paul again. No luck.

I was never, never scared, doing all I did on my own. I just kept my head down and would only study my map in the stall of a restroom because I wanted to belong and not look like a tourist. However, after a couple of months of doing it every weekend by myself, I have to admit, I got kind of lonely.

So, I decided to go to the "meet and greet" event that the nanny agency had every week at the Paramus Mall. It was an opportunity for you to meet other nannies, get their stories, or maybe share some helpful advice on how to help out the family.

Not me, I went there on a mission; my goal was to see which one of these damn nannies wanted to go to Manhattan with me on the weekends. I met a couple of very cool girls. Their families were seriously messed up and made my family look normal-*if* that was even possible.

These two girls wanted to go to the city with me, but they were always on lockdown and never allowed to use their families' cars-unless it was for the nanny mall adventure on Wednesday nights. Gag!

I pulled out three maps of the city, which I always carried with me, and showed them where I had been and what I had done. I assured them that it would be okay. Desperate for company, I pleaded with them, "Come on! We can do this, girls. We could use public transportation, meet up, and then ride into the city together."

Believe me, convincing these two girls to do this was the most challenging thing that had ever come my way. For Heaven's sake, one didn't even use tampons because her mother told her they were for "dirty girls." Good Lord, I thought I was sheltered! But, they did go, and we had a fabulous time each time we went. I had to coach them, however, on not wearing too much color if they wanted properly to blend in like a true New Yorker.

Well, it was Wednesday night; it was time to go to the mall for our gathering. I stopped at a shoe store for the mom I worked for, to see if her shoes were in yet. When I turned around, there, standing in the cashmere coat, trying on shoes, was Mr. Wonderful himself. Yes, the beautiful guy from the airplane. I knew he saw me, but he looked right through me. He didn't know who in the hell I was.

Racing over to the food court to find my nanny posse, I told them, "Get up! We are going on a stake out!" I quickly explained to them, as I walked with my uncover strut behind this man, that I knew this guy and needed to be near this guy and that they were going to help me–no matter what.

These girls were fascinated by my theatrical drama. They usually stared at me when I said anything. Then would look at each other like, *Oh, my stars*! I was the third wheel, but in my mind, I was teaching these girls to become independent and free women.

We followed my mysterious fascination all around the mall. We did a giant loop, until we ended back at the food court. A Suzy-homemaker-of-a-nanny spotted us and started screaming all our names out, telling us to come and see the macramé holder things she was teaching the other nannies how to make.

He suddenly stopped and turned around on his heels and said to me, "So, do you want to tell me why you are following me?" He was smiling and speaking perfect English. His dark eyes held me in a trance, a mesmerizing trance that, even to this day, I cannot begin to explain.

The other two bolted, heading for Suzy and leaving me there to fend for myself. Then, he said something to me in Arabic. I still did not say a word. I later learned that he called me "beautiful bright eyes." He put his hand out and introduced himself, "Hello, my name is Javi." He smiled when I didn't shake his hand back.

I stood there and said, "I am sorry that I was following you. You probably don't remember me. I met you at the Detroit airport. Well, we didn't meet; we rode the same plane from Detroit to New York. I like your coat." I laugh to this day, thinking, *Really, Christine? That was as good as you could do?*

"Interesting." There was a very long pause as he stood and stared at me. "Would you like to get a drink?" he asked, putting his hand on his chin and still staring inquisitively at me.

All I could feel was, *Boom!* My mind felt like it could possibly explode. *He wants to have a drink? With me?* I was panicking and worrying. I was only eighteen! I could not drink. Then I was thinking, *Cool, you can drink at the mall? No, wait. He will think I am a naive baby if I tell him I didn't know you could order a drink at the mall!*

I think he sensed my panic, probably because I said, "*Drink?*" like a crazy person.

"How about some coffee. Do you like coffee?" He didn't even wait for me to respond; he just put his hand on the small of my back and paraded me towards a little coffee stand.

"So, do you want to tell me your name?" he asked as he looked over and smiled at me. I was so intimidated by his beauty. He looked so mysterious, so handsome. He smelled good, and he had impeccable manners. Plus, his hands were perfectly manicured.

Okay, here is a weird little side tip about me. I love men's hands. It's usually is the first thing I look at when I meet any man. First, because hands are what hold you and make you feel loved and wanted. Second, you can tell a lot about a man by his hands.

"My name is Christine; it's very nice to meet you, Javi." He drew back, put his hand on his heart, and said, "Icing on the cake. How can your name be just as beautiful as you?"

Forget about it. I was hooked. The two of us sat and talked about quite a bit, until security started turning off the lights in the food court. He walked me to my car that night and asked if he could see me again. Then he thanked me for stalking him, and he leaned in to give me a hug.

I used to challenge my memory from that night, trying to remember every detail. He only asked me about me. I barely knew anything about him. However, he was the most interesting person I had met since the wheels of my plane touched down on this far-away soil.

Heck, I was used to frat boys who didn't know how to treat a woman. Their idea of good manners was to honk only one time in my driveway when they came to pick me up. Although, my father did tell me one time, "If that dick honks for you one more time, I will break his legs. NO boy honks for my daughter. Do you understand me, Christine?"

After talking every night on the phone until two am, Javi asked if he could take me on a date. Friday at five pm, he waited at the end of my driveway in a brand new black Audi. It had very dark tinted windows and shiny wheels. It was like nothing I was used to being picked up in.

When I looked out the curtains of the home I was now starting to despise, I remember saying out loud, "Jackpot." It bothers me so much when I think back; I was ridiculous about material things. I try to cut myself some slack, though, because I was under a spell, a dangerous spell.

"So, my queen, what do you say we go into the city, have dinner, and meet some of my friends? Are you ready for the time of your life?" He flashed me his perfect Moroccan grin, took my hand, and laced his fingers in mine–a very bold move, I thought.

Where do I start? Queen, city–wait, back up, "*my* queen," leather interior, friends, duel exhaust Audi, and surround sound speakers playing my favorite song. *He remembered my favorite song?* His smile was enough, but now he was handing me a gift.

"Open it. That night when I noticed you stalking me (he laughs), I saw you trying to look at jewelry instead of me. I went back the next day and asked the jeweler what you tried on. Please tell me he got it right. I want to give you something special, to remember that night," he said, smiling his perfect grin at me and tapping his steering wheel to the beat of the song that filled the car.

Holy shit, are you kidding me? My hands trembled as I rubbed the fuzzy, chocolate-colored jewelry box. In all the years I had been alive, I had never received jewelry expensive enough to be in a box like this.

I think he sensed I was nervous, so he reached over and touched my cheek and said, "Hey, hey. Please open it. I have been waiting all week for you to open that box. Make me a happy man; please open it. I have been waiting to see that smile of yours." Then he leaned over me to fasten my seat belt for me.

"Okay, but I will tell you if it isn't *the one*," I said, winking to him. He smiled back at me, winking, as if to say, *Of course.*

It was the exact one, and I could not hold back my tears. I missed the whole drive into the city because I was crying. He finally turned off the road and parked the car. He was a nervous wreck; apparently, he was not used to boohooing young girls in his front seat.

"Christine, please look at me," he said, as he took my chin in his hand.

"I want to tell you something." He began wiping my tears very tenderly with a tissue, but they would not stop flowing.

"Shhhhh. Please don't cry. You are very special to me. I love the way you make me feel. You are not scared to be yourself around me, but I could not wait to see you tonight. I want to shower you with everything you deserve, and I will spend a lifetime making sure of this. If that's okay with you," he said, leaning his head back on the headrest of his seat, closing his eyes.

"Javi, I am crying because no one has ever given me such a gift-ever. Especially not a guy. And, it is *the* bracelet. The jeweler pretty much snapped the bracelet back out of my hands when I told him I was 'just looking' that night. I said to my girlfriends as we left the store, 'If a guy ever gives you a bracelet like that, ladies, remind yourself how lucky you are-everyday.' Plus, it is the most romantic thing I could possibly dream of."

I looked down at my breathtaking gift and watched the diamonds sparkle from the light that shimmered through the car window as other cars drove by. Looking at it, I knew what excepting this bracelet would mean.

"Christine?" he leaned very close to me, "I am not some guy. Baby, please look at me." As I looked up, he kissed me. At first, gently on my forehead and then he slowly moved on to both of my wet cheeks. Then he kissed my eyes, my wet lashes. Pausing, he looked into my eyes. Then he moved to my mouth. One word: Heaven.

"Who in the heck is Javi?" I heard my daughter pipe up from behind me. I immediately started laughing. I was typing away in my bedroom, with my ear buds in. I didn't hear her until she leaned in and shouted, "Mom!"

"Oh, hey, Em," I said to her, quickly closing down my chapter of the never-talked-about Javi.

"Does Dad know about this guy?" she asked me, tapping her foot and scowling at me.

"What the heck, Emily Ann? Don't be silly! Of course he does!" Truth be told, I was nervous about pulling all these old feelings back up. Not only is this memory twenty-five (plus) years old, but every time Ed used to ask about Javi, I always blew it off and told Ed, "He was a stupid douche bag. Don't ever worry about him." Truth be told, I worried about bringing up all this stuff. I can only hope Ed will remember it's the past.

Let's just put it this way: it was a whirlwind romance. Javi was very affectionate. He really listened to my every word. He took me all over the place. Every Friday, he would be waiting for me at five o'clock sharp. I would get in the car, and he would hand me a new sparkly gift of some sort.

Then he would take me to the theater or clothes and shoe shopping. We went to the Statue of Liberty, ice skating in Rockefeller Center, and to the Bronx Zoo. We did everything and anything I wanted. We would take long walks in Central Park and lie on a blanket for hours as I read to him. We went to little restaurants in China Town after going to art galleries. We went to nightclubs and danced all night, just the two of us.

My lunch in the Twin Towers was with Javi, and it's one of my all-time favorite memories. But honestly, it was not really having lunch with him. He left for a meeting that lasted most of the lunch. Leaning in and kissing me, he called the waiter over and explained to him that I was to be taken care of and that I better not look around, wanting or waiting for anything. I was ticked off he made such a show, but the way he kissed me erased any trace of my anger within seconds.

It was an amazing lunch because of the people, the view, and the building. I even asked the waiter to sit down with me. He stood and talked with me the entire time, so I told him he might as well sit down with me. Plus, he was really funny. I had a huge pizza, and I didn't want to eat alone.

When he refused to sit with me, I asked to see the manager. I explained to the manager that I was writing an article for *W Magazine* and that I needed the waiter's perspective on how wonderful the Towers were. I told him I was calling the article, "It's Better Than Home: My Love for the Twin Towers." The manager then waved my new friend over, and we had an unbelievable meal. I never laughed so hard with anyone-not even Daren!

I never saw him again. I worried desperately for my friend Ryan, as I watched with an aching heart, the day the Towers crashed. I was praying on my knees in my bedroom for my angel Ryan, wondering if he still worked there. To this day, on the wall next to my bed, there hangs a little pink cross with the tiny name *Ryan*.

Lastly-and I think you are waiting for this next part-Javi and I did have amazing, earth-shattering sex. Yes, it was the kind of sex that made you drunk with love-or what I thought was love. I was so young. I find myself thinking again, *I was the same age then as my son is now!* This thought gives me head-to-toe shivers. Blah!

We would stay in the city all day, go to his friend's apartment in midtown to change, and then we would go out for the second part of our day together. We would go to parties, where almost the entire room was filled with men. Most of the people who attended these parties were of the same background as Javi, speaking in Arabic all night. To be honest, I usually found a nice, friendly waitress to talk to. I still wanted to know all I could about being a girl in the city.

The girls that attended these parties were young, white girls like me, escorted by very handsome Middle Eastern men. These women never spoke to me, though. I would try, you know, to make trivial conversation, anything! But, what I usually got in return was nothing–until the day I met Cyndi.

I saw her standing in the bathroom at a party in a very fancy hotel that Javi had taken me to in the city. I told her I loved her fur and that my grandma had a coat made of rabbit. She smiled at me, as I rolled my eyes as if to say, *"Yep, rabbit–really."* Then she handed me her cherry-red lipstick.

"Put it on; it will make Javi crazy," she said as she lit a cigarette and winced as the smoke floated up, stinging her eyes.

Doing as instructed, I watched her smoking from the reflection of the mirror. *How did this woman know Javi?* That thought was all that raced through my mind.

"You know Javi?" I asked, trying not to sound threatened by her stunning older beauty. Now by older, I mean you could tell this chic knew what she was doing in the sack. Let's just say, when I say *older*, I mean sexually experienced.

"Mmmm-hmmm. I do," she said to me as took a drag of her cigarette. As she moved herself to the bathroom counter, I watched her as she ashed in the sink. She offered me a cigarette, so I took one. She was surprised I knew how to inhale and not cough.

"Wow, you know what you are doing with that cigarette. Better not let Javi know you smoke." She now looked at me as if she was somewhat impressed.

"I don't smoke, but my friend Daren and I practiced smoking a lot," I explained, thinking to myself how good this cigarette tasted and how much I missed Daren.

"Cut the bullshit. How do you know Javi?" I asked her, leaning into her space as I ashed in the sink too. I was thinking, *Maybe Marlboros give me an edge!*

"Take it easy. Everyone knows Javi. Everyone has heard about this mysterious Christine that he is obsessed with. So, you are the girl that has put a spell over him?" She started laughing and snorting. Then she actually started pointing at me while she tapped her lighter on the counter with her other hand.

"Who is everyone? And what in the hell is so funny?" I asked, leaning against the wall directly in front of her. She would have to touch me if she wanted down. *Oh, Lord help her if she even touches me.* This thought played through my mind as I scowled at her.

"Nothing. I can see he really does pick well," she said, giving me the yeah-I-am-checking-you-out stare. She was scanning my body from head to toe.

I finished the last drag, and I blew it into her face. I never took my eyes off her as I wet my fingers in the cool tap water and pinched off the end of my cigarette. Then I turned and shot it directly into the toilet, sending her a non-verbal message: *Bitch, do not mess with me.* Then I grabbed my purse off the counter and headed to the door to find Javi.

"Hey, wait. Christine?" Cyndi called, not even looking at me; she was leaning over the sink. We stood there, looking at each other in the reflection of the mirror. "Javi will always need me, but try to remember, little girl, that you are just his Green Card, his ticket to America." Then she broke her stare in the mirror, turned to me, and gave me the bye-bye wave.

I raced to the exit of the hotel, finding myself standing on the curb in a darkness that consumed me. I was not familiar with where we were. For the first time in eight months, I wanted to go home. I actually said out loud, screaming, "I hate this city!" I think maybe we were in Uptown, but I didn't recognize anything. I was standing there, freezing, semi-drunk, so young, and so very far away from home. I remember saying to myself, *Green Card,* over and over.

Javi came running up to me from behind, trying to hug me as I wiggled free. He was trying to keep me from hailing a cab, but I was screaming bloody murder at him, "Get away from me, Javi!" He stood back, saying very softly, "What happened in there?"

"I will tell you what happened, Javi. There's a whore in the bathroom who apparently knows you," I said to him as I did air quotes, when I said *knows you.*

"Oh, and by the way, she said that you need her, but I am only your Green Card. How about that?" I was standing fully erect, with my arm in the air to hail a cab. Now I was crying, a complete jet-black mess. The nine coats of mascara I let the woman at Macy's put on me was now running all over my face. My new, beautiful white cashmere gloves looked like I had rubbed them all over the subway wall.

"You must be talking about Cyndi. Am I right? She is just jealous of your youth and your beauty. She shoved her hands down my pants one night, and I pushed her away. Then I told her to keep her nasty hands off me," he said, trying again to approach me.

"What about the Green Card bullshit she gave me? Is that true?" Holding my ground and looking at him with fury, I took off my new gloves flung them into the road, one by one, and watched traffic drive over them. I stood with my back to him again.

"Why would you say that? How do you know I wouldn't want you to live with me in Morocco someday?" Javi whispered as he gently twirled me around, smoothing his hands around my waist. He continued on, kissing my hands and telling me he would never betray me like that.

I half believed him, but there was a new scar on my heart that I wasn't used to feeling with him. The new scar was doubt.

The next evening, I was feeding and bathing kids that weren't mine so that the parents could go to *another* important meeting. Watching as they drove off again in separate cars, the doorbell rang. There was a man dressed in what looked like a waiter's uniform. He asked me my name. When I told him, he handed me a little turquoise box.

I went over and sat down on the bi-level steps. I carefully untied the beautiful silk ribbon and gingerly opened the box. My hands were shaking. I may be from a backwards town in Ohio, but come on, every girl knows what a Tiffany & Co. box looks like! Sitting inside the box were two perfect diamond-studded earrings. I snapped it back shut because I thought I was dreaming. Just then, the doorbell rang again.

I went to open the door, and it was a different courier. He asked me my name. I responded, and he handed me an envelope. I sat back down on the stairs, studying the envelope and wondering what it was. I set my little box down next to me and opened the envelope. It was a note:

Dear Christine,

My heart has never felt such pain as it did last night. Just the thought of you leaving me fills me with sadness. I am sorry you had to go through that last night.

Yours,

Javi

xoxo

Under the letter were two tickets to Morocco. Then the phone rang. "Hey, lady, did you get any mail today?" Javi asked me, laughing.

"Would you be talking about these little diamonds I think some guy sent me? Hey, you wouldn't happen to have a magnifying glass, would you?" I started laughing and so did he. "Javi, they are too much, too, too much!" Reopening the box to stare at their impeccable beauty, I was again impressed.

"I can't wait to see you in them. What about the tickets? Will you go with me this summer?" he asked, as the kids got up, asking me loudly if their mommy was home yet.

"Ummm, yes, I would love to go to Morocco. Is that a trick question?" He could hear I had to go, so he said, "Christine, sleep tight. Please know my heart will belong to you forever. I love you." And he hung up. I just sat in total shock. I did not move from those steps for close to an hour.

I eventually became very jaded with all his gifts. He lavished me with so many things. He was a little overprotective, too. He would get really ticked off if I talked to another guy–no matter where we were. Really, even if it was the checkout guy at Radio Shack, he would take my hand in his hands and finish my conversation for me. I just thought it was one of the weird oddities about him.

One weekend, I could not spend time with him. I was going to Lake George to ski with the family I lived with. I forgot to mention, the dad had started really snooping around about Javi and me, asking me questions.

When I told Javi over the phone that the dad I worked for kept asking about him, he literally hung up the phone. I thought he was pissed. I thought, *Okay, fine. Talk to you later.*

Wrong. He was standing at my front door thirty minutes later, telling me he wanted to meet the dad. I didn't even realize how insane the whole thing was until days later.

"Go get him!" Javi spoke in a tone I was not familiar with–at all. He could tell by my look that I wasn't moving, so he grabbed my arm and gently pulled me out to the front porch.

"Christine, I don't need him to ever wonder who I am. I am none of his business. Besides, I want to meet this man that lives in the same house as you. You know what? I don't want you living here anymore! You can stay with me, and I will bring you over in the mornings."

I asked, "What about your school?" He had told me he was a student. He didn't answer me; he just turned from me and went into the house. He stood in the foyer until I went and got the dad.

They spoke for about fifteen or so minutes. At first it was very casual chitchat. Then, Javi asked him how long he had lived here, the name of the firm he worked at, and where he grew up. Javi always added little side comments to the dad's answers, like, "Oh, cool firm; do you know so and so?" And the dad did know so and so.

Weird, it was like he was enjoying himself. This confused the hell out of me. Then Javi asked all about the ski trip, where we were staying, and such. I thought it was a normal conversation. They were smiling at each other. Hell, the dad answered every question and even asked Javi if he wanted a drink. I did not realize, at the time, that Javi was interviewing him.

"Can you walk me to my car?" Javi asked me. As he leaned in and grinned at me, he graciously told the dad, "Goodnight, sir." Out in the driveway, he asked me to get in his car. I was thinking to myself, *Okay, no problem.*

Once I settled in the front seat, he turned to me and said, "Do not make eye contact with that man. He is hideous and disgusting. Please, Christine, you promise me. I do not like the way he looks at you! Go get your stuff; you are coming home with me." He leaned over me, opened my door, and pointed for me to get out.

"What do I tell them, Javi? Those kids need me." Standing there confused, I was getting mad at his orders.

"Don't say anything to *him* except that I will bring you home in the morning. Go, or I will pack your shit for you!" I thought, *Oh, man! He is in trouble.* He didn't know it, but our first "real" fight was coming down his pipe! I stood and counted down out loud: five, four, three, two, one, *SLAM*! I slammed his car door with all my might and ran up to the house.

The next morning, I left for Lake George with the family. The kids were excited, and I was happy to be doing fun stuff with them. Over time, we had started growing on each other. The little one actually adored me. I let her sleep with me almost every night. This was usually because her parents were always screaming at each other. I used to sing little nursery rhymes to her or have her bunny tell us about its day while she was at school. She must be almost twenty-five years old now! Sorry, reader. I am digressing!

Here I insert an intermission for you, my dear reader. Please, go to the bathroom or pop some popcorn. The Javi ending is almost here, and I promise you will not want to move for this one.

It was a long, two-hour car ride; I sat and starred out the window as the kids sang "99 Bottles of Beer." The mom didn't come with us, which was fine with me. We could all use a tension-free weekend. I, however, knew I would never be able to tell Javi that it had been just the dad and me for the entire weekend.

The cabin was more like a wilderness lodge. The kids and I had a blast! We did everything possible within the first three hours of being there. Exhausted from all the family fun, I decided to go and check out the town. I thought I might find something to buy or sit down somewhere and enjoy the quiet.

Finding an adorable little gift shop, a boutique, I noticed a foreign-looking man standing, oh, about fifty feet from the door I exited. Trust me. I noticed all men who resembled Javi, but I didn't think anything of it. I kept walking and found a café. I went in and found a booth. Just then, another man, resembling the same man I just saw five minutes ago, came in and sat down in a booth behind me.

Heading back to my cabin paradise, I stopped to turn around. I just had this feeling I was being watched. Nope, no one was behind me. *Silly girl,* was all I kept telling myself as I picked up my pace to get home, never looking back again.

The next day, we went out to lunch and later made an enormous bonfire. We all cooked a huge meal together for dinner. I watched the dad, trying to figure out what Javi was talking about. I trusted my instincts, so I thought, *Let me see if I notice anything.* He *did* laugh at everything I said. He was always telling the kids to mind me. Occasionally, he would touch me, but it was usually to hand me something.

Nothing had my freak radar up. Except, that night he started drinking–drinking a lot. The kids thought he was funny; I was just worried he would puke, and I would have to clean it up.

Taking another break from the exhausting family fun, I went into the kitchen to find the phone. I missed Javi and wanted to tell him that I was sorry. When I called, it just rang off the hook; no one answered. I wasn't surprised; he was never home. The dad came into the kitchen to get the hidden liquor on the top shelf of a cupboard to pour another drink.

"Hey, I was talking to my coworker the other day about your Javi," he said, slurring his words. "You know, his old man is worth millions and millions and millions! Did you know that? You lucked out, little girl." He kept laughing, repeating, "My nanny is going to be a millionaire someday. How do you like that?

The problem was that I did not know any of that. *What in the hell? I will try to call him one more time.* I let it ring probably thirty times. When I finally heard hello, it was a woman's voice. I hung up. Well, actually, I slammed the phone on the counter about five or six times and then I hung up. I just kept saying to myself, *Christine, you stupid little girl!*

Deciding to round up the kids in the family room, I made them all beds on the couches and let them watch TV. They were absolutely thrilled! It was ten o'clock, and they were happily surprised to get television. I kissed them all goodnight and asked each one to help me pack up their stuff in the morning. If I was going to spoil them, they had to be my little helpers. They all screamed, "Deal!" as I climbed the stairs to find my bedroom.

Taking a delicious, candle-lit bubble bath in a clawfoot tub, I sat and soaked as I thought about Javi. I was contemplating whether to buy his bullshit excuse when he tries to explain about that woman answering the phone. I was thinking to myself, *Where does he go all the time? He is always going to meetings, but I thought he was a student. Why didn't he tell me his father was loaded? Hell, where did I think the money was coming from?*

Completely tired, I wrapped myself in my terry cloth robe and tried to get some sleep in the enormous bed. The dad let me have the master since his wife stayed home. Drifting off to sleep, I awoke to a heaviness on top of me. As I opened my eyes, it was black, but I could smell whiskey.

"What the fuck do you want? Get off me!" I screamed at the suffocating black shadow on top of me as I struggled underneath his weight. He put his hand over my mouth and told me not to move. Then he kept saying he was sorry, that he didn't know why he was acting like this.

"It's because you are drunk! Get off me!" I screamed through his hand as I dug my nails into his flesh. He kept calling me by his wife's name! All I could think was, *Please, God, help me. Please don't let this man rape me.* He put his hands around my neck, squeezing so tightly, saying her name again. He tried to enter inside of me, but there was strength in me that I never knew existed. I rolled to my side and pulled and clawed my way the edge of the bed, but he grabbed my legs and pulled me back to him. He was on his knees now, so I kicked him square in the chest, which sent him flying off the bed.

I did not move; I just got my bearings in case he came back at me. Deciding to slip off the bed, towards the door, I fled down the steps into the kitchen. I never looked back to see if he was chasing me. Once in the kitchen, I started throwing open every drawer to find a knife–a big knife.

I went to the tiny bathroom in the back of the kitchen, locked the door, and sat down on the floor holding my huge knife. I also started throwing up everywhere because I could smell him on me, and I could not believe I was almost raped.

I think I passed out because the next thing I heard was a little taping on the other side of the door. A little voice said to me, "Christine, Daddy made us pancakes. Do you want some?"

Looking into the mirror, I was horrified. I had a giant bruise on the right side of my neck. And I had puke in my hair. I just bent over the sink and washed my hair with hand soap. I actually washed my entire body in that sink. I didn't want to leave the room.

Peeking out the door, I didn't see anyone around, so I slipped out of the bathroom. Then I heard a voice from behind me say, "Hey, there you are. No hard feelings about last night, right? Guess I can't hold my booze." He said this while holding his palms up, shrugging his shoulders, and giving me a goofy smile.

I wasn't sure if I heard him correctly, so I turned to look at him and said, "What? Are you kidding me?" He just started saying that he knows better than to drink shots of whisky and he was sorry. He said that it's a good thing we are both grown ups who can keep our mouths shut. I left him talking to himself in the kitchen. I kept thinking, *Fucker, you are going to be so, so sorry.*

The car ride home felt long. I sat in the back with all the kids, which thrilled them. However, they knew something was wrong. I just told them, as he looked at me in the rearview mirror, "No, kids, don't worry. I have a tummy ache. I had a very bad dream last night."

I plotted in the car that night about how I would pack all my stuff and leave as soon as I could get in touch with Javi. Trying hard not to cry, I was close to tears thinking about how attached these kids had gotten to me.

I went straight to my cell in the basement. My room was actually a basement workshop they had turned into a bedroom. I started packing everything, happy that I had saved all the boxes from the new stereo I just got.

Seeing a receipt on the floor, I realized I had to pick up a speaker I bought from the mall. Grabbing my boxes and leaving so much behind, I grabbed the car keys to the car they let me drive. I locked up my cell tight as a drum and took off.

I realized that I had acquired tons of junk since I had been here, stuff Javi wouldn't want around. My stereo and personal stuff I could send to my mom. Finding a pay phone, I called my mom to let her know Fed Ex would be delivering some boxes. "Mom, is that you?" She, of course, was worried by my call and asked if I was okay. Resting my head against the disgusting receiver, I paused, trying so hard not to start weeping. "Yeah, Mom, thanks. All good. I love you."

I hung up on her. I felt so bad for doing that. But my insides were screaming, and I knew she would know something by my voice if I kept talking.

Standing in line at Stereo City, waiting for my speaker, I heard a man behind me say my name. I turned around, but I didn't recognize him. He asked if he could have a moment of my time.

As I looked over, I saw the same man from the diner earlier. But, he had on a black jacket now, just like the man escorting me into the back room. He honestly looked like a criminal.

"Sure. Everything is okay?" I asked. I was thinking, *What in the hell is this about?* He asked me to sit down, and then he did not say another word until his notebook was in front of him. He clicked his pen and wrote the date and time.

"Christine, do you know a man named Javi ------?" (Sorry, reader. I cannot give a real name.)

"Yes, yes I do. Is he okay?" I asked as my voice crackled. Looking around the office, I noticed the guy from the diner was standing in the doorway, with the door closed behind him, looking straight ahead.

"Christine, we advise you to stay away from him. Do not ever make contact with him again. Do not answer him if he tries to contact you. Do you understand? Do you agree with what we are asking of you?" I was thinking to myself, *No, I do not understand.*

He kept talking, and my head felt like a balloon. I could see his lips moving, but I was not absorbing a single word. So, I squeezed my eyes shut and shook my head. "Who exactly is *we* anyways?" I asked him, reopening my eyes to look down at his paper to see what he was writing. It was my name that he kept circling, over and over.

"The Federal Bureau of Investigation, Christine, the FBI." Then he leaned in and said very quietly, almost in a whisper, "We know you are a good girl, Christine. Off the record, Christine, please don't go back." He patted the top of my hand as he looked directly into my eyes.

Then he asked me to sign a piece of paper before I left the room. I do not even know what I signed. I remember leaving the room thinking, *Oh, my God. Oh, my God. Please help me; I am just a little girl from Ohio. How did I get involved in this?* In a complete haze, I walked down the cement hallway for mall employees only.

Before I went home, and I do not know why I did this, I went to Javi's apartment in the neighboring town. I knew I was probably being followed or watched. I didn't care; I needed to see his face one more time.

I hung out in the car a couple of minutes and looked around before I snuck out of my car. I moved in calculated steps, hopping in all the shadows that were cast onto the sidewalk from the night sky. Reaching to find his key on the top of the door ledge, I could feel the cold metal on my fingertips. I slipped it into my hand and quietly opened the front door.

I slowly went up the tiny staircase and around the corner into his kitchen. I could immediately hear voices. I went over to his bedroom, and I knocked. I don't know why I knocked, either. I think I knew who was behind that door. I think mentally I couldn't take any more drama-without ending up in a mental institution.

Resting my head on the door, I took a deep breath and said, "Javi, please come out here." I heard scuffling and a woman's voice, so I decided to open the door. And, yes, folks, there was Cyndi, half naked.

Javi ran up to me and shoved me out into the kitchen-not forcefully, but like he was shooing me.

"Hey, it's not what you think. Please sit and let me explain," Javi pleaded with me as he rocked back and forth holding his robe shut. The look on his face said it all; he knew he was screwed.

"Javi, I don't give shit who you sleep with anymore. I just came to give you these back," I said softly as I handed him my earrings and bracelet. Remembering he also gave me a necklace, I pulled my hair back to undo the clasp. That's when he saw the bruise on my neck.

"What the? Christine?" He held my wrist tightly. Holding my arm in the air, Javi looked into my eyes and said in a thundering tone, "Please, Christine, tell me. Did he do this to you? Tell me, please."

He held my face gently in his hands. I watched his eyes water and turn into a horrid, tortured sea of black. When he touched my neck, I winced. This made him moan in sympathetic agony, grabbing his own hair.

All I could do was nod. I was exhausted. I handed him the necklace, which he threw against the wall. He went over, picked up the phone, and spoke in Arabic into the receiver. Then he disappeared to change out of his cheating robe, a robe I had bought him a week ago.

Not even five minutes later, about five men showed up in the kitchen. They all started screaming in Arabic, pointing at my neck, and pacing.

He came back over to me, which made me back up against the wall in fear. He stopped in front of me, his hands hovering over my body. He looked at me with shock. I was moving away from him, not towards him. He took my hands in his, closed his eyes, and chanted something under his breath. As he tried to kiss my hands, I coiled my fingers into tight balls.

Desperately, he said, "I will be back. Will you please wait for me? Please, look at me. Please, tell me you love me." All I did was point at the bedroom door.

"I will take care of *her*, baby. Will you wait for me. Please?" Then he turned and said something to his friend in Arabic, which sent him to the bedroom to get the whore out of the house.

She spit at me as she went out through the kitchen. Javi drew his fist back at her face and then grabbed the kitchen chair, as if he was going to hurl it. He stopped and looked over at me, changing his mind; instead, he clenched the chair that rocked with his white-knuckle fury. When Cyndi was out of sight, I am pretty sure I heard the man who was physically removing her from the house start smacking her. Hearing those noises put my stomach in knots, and the room began to spin.

"Wait here, please, my love," Javi said as he put one of my palms on his face, kissing the palm of my other hand. I simply nodded, and he turned and left with his friends.

I sat down at the kitchen table, put my hands over my ears, and put my head down on the table. It was as if I could hear someone screaming.

I realized it was me. My mind was screaming: *Get out. Get out. Get out. GET OUT!* I swear it felt like I was having a nervous breakdown. If I didn't know better, I would have believed a force was physically moving me. It was almost like my guardian angel grabbed my shirt collar that night.

I did get out. I ran down the steps and stood in the dark shadows on the sidewalk for a moment. I wanted to make sure I didn't see Javi and his friends. I did see a K-car. My grandma D had that same car. We used to joke that she looked like FBI. I went over to the door and knocked on the window. The stranger rolled it down. All I said to him was, "I need help." The stranger got out and opened the door to the backseat for me. It was a cop; he kept showing me his badge. I told him, "I don't care if you are the mailman, buddy. No disrespect, but I just need to get out of here."

"Take me to any Holiday Inn that is far away, please." Those were the only words I spoke the entire care ride. Sitting on the hotel bed that night, I placed a call. I knew I could no longer trust any man—except my father and Daren. So, I called my oldest and dearest friend.

"Hey, Daren. It's me. Are you up for a road trip? If I get some money and send it to you, will you come and get me?" I begged him through my tears, completely hoarse from crying hysterically.

"Andi, I am already backing down the driveway. Where am I going?" Daren asked me in a hushed tone. He asked me to please stop crying or he would start crying.

I never heard from Javi ever again, nor did the nanny agency ever try to contact me—neither did the family I worked for. I literally fell off the grid. It was time to reinvent Christine. I had rolled to the bottom of my bright and shiny mountain. Christine's Kilimanjaro was on fire.

Little side note: I know not all men behave like the men portrayed in this chapter. Plus, I know for a fact all men who speak Arabic do not behave like this. I do, however, think New Yorkers are the kindest people I have ever met. Someday, I will go back there with the people I love, my family.

FAITH, LITTLE GIRL 12

I returned home to Ohio, to the bedroom of my childhood home. I needed to feel safe and pick up the pieces to my shattered heart. Most days, very depressing music could be heard floating from my hiding place.

"Christine! You have a phone call!" I heard my mother shout up the stairs to my bedroom, or my "grief cave" as I called it.

My parents were so used to my melodrama that I never had to tell them why I was really back home. When they asked, I said, "The family was nuts and exhausting." When I explained my long list of daily chores, it was enough of a reason for my mother. Heck, my mother made my bed until I moved out on my own, so the very idea of me cleaning another woman's house left her laughing. She dropped the conversation.

"Hello?" There was nothing but silence on the other end of the phone. "Hello?" Again, silence. If I stayed on the line long enough, I could eventually hear breathing. But no one ever spoke. Ever. I would always slam the phone down, screaming obscenities.

My mother would shout at me, "Christine! You're not in New York anymore! Stop talking like that! And quit slamming my phone around, or you will have to buy me a new one. In case you forgot, you don't have a job! Guess what? Phones are expensive, Christine!"

I would ask her, "Mom, was it a man's voice on the phone?"

She would reply, "Man? I don't know about any man. Why on earth would a *man* be calling you, Christine?" I would just cover my ears and go back to my grief cave.

I spent a lot of time starring off into space. I think I actually looked at the same spot on my wall for two days straight. Plus, I was no idiot. I was pretty sure that it was Javi calling me. Although he never spoke, it was still driving me mad–like, literally crazy. I had stopped sleeping, eating, bathing, laughing, or speaking. Plus, I became paranoid. I would only go outside if it was pitch-dark.

"Hey, your dad let me up. Hello? Christine?" Daren said to me as he leaned over my curled-up body. "Christine, cut the shit. It's over. Move on!" But all I could think was, *Wow, he said my actual name.* Rolling over on my little mattress, I faced the wall, hoping he would leave.

One night at two am, I had convinced myself to disassemble my bed. I was actually scared to sleep in my bed next to the window, so my mattress was on the floor. I watched Daren sitting at my vanity, throwing my old makeup into the tiny trashcan that was filled with crumpled, snotty tissues. My sacred vanity, how I loved it. Thinking back now, it was probably my favorite thing my parents gave me in my entire life.

"Daren, can I ask you something?" I said to him, sitting up in my bed. I was actually woozy; I don't know how long I had been lying around. I had lost track of the days.

"Wow, what do you know? She's alive! The crypt keeper speaks!" Daren said, laughing at his own joke as he lathered on my lip gloss, puckering at his reflection in the mirror, rolling his eyes to the ceiling.

"What am I going to do?" I paused. "Daren, I am so scared," I said as I re-covered my head under the sheets that were so dirty they could probably stand on their own in the corner. I refused to allow my mother to wash them, for fear I would loose his scent forever. I kept one of his t-shirts, which smelled just like him. I kept it stuffed in my pillow case. I still loved his smell.

I heard Daren come over to me, and he sat down next to my sad little mattress on the floor. He was now lying on top of me, squishing me with sporadic rounds of play slapping and tickling, as he held the sheets tight over my head. I started laughing as he told me how bad I stunk. I stopped and realized, *Hey, I just laughed!*

"Christine Marie, you are sacred of what? That stupid asshole in New Jersey? Please, he is pathetic! He doesn't have the balls to cross the Ohio line to come and find you!" Daren said this in a matter-of-fact tone, like I should already know it. He went back over to my vanity to put on my mascara.

"Look, Andi, he would have already been here. Don't you think? If he wanted you back? He would be at your door. Wake up; he never gave a shit about you! Stupid pig, if he were here, I would snap his neck!" He looked at his reflection, practicing his different smiles, while wagging his finger at me.

Daren went to my bedroom window, screamed, and threw himself on my bedroom floor, as if he saw something out the window. I, of course, started screaming, saying, "What? What!" Covering myself back up, I was now worrying about what he saw out the window. It could be my worst nightmare! Daren started rolling on my floor, laughing hysterically and pointing at me. I still didn't realize what he was doing or talking about.

"Christine! You are crazy! You have dropped off the deep end! Stop this! No one is out there!" I started shaking my head in disbelief from under the covers. He went over to the window and pulled back the curtain. "Uncover your smelly head. *LOOK*, Christine! It's just the idiot next door mowing his grass!" He came back over and ripped the sheets off me.

"Damn it! This is enough!" Daren screamed at me and was now holding my legs, dragging my body across my bedroom floor as I wiggled and flailed about. He ended up jumping on top of me, and we rolled around, wrestling, until my mother screamed bloody murder up the stairs. "What's going on up there?" she demanded. Daren ended up pulling my hair to get me to be still.

"Ouch, okay! You know I don't like hair pulling!" I said in a sad little voice, panting. That tussle was the most exercise I had gotten in an entire month.

Not convinced I wouldn't move again, he straddled me, which was a huge mistake. Flashbacks of the dad straddling me in the dark still haunted me, causing me too many sleepless nights. This position *did* send me off the deep end! I remember pushing Daren back as if he were a piece of cardboard, slamming him straight on his back against the floor. "Don't you ever! Ever! Sit on me like that!" I screamed, with a crazed look on my face.

Now I was crying. Daren knew there were some things I could not yet talk about. He knew, as I was lying there curled into a ball, I was broken. For the first time since we traveled from New Jersey, he looked truly worried for me. We lay side by side on the floor, crying together. Holding hands, we did not speak a word to each other. He stayed next to me, wiping my tears away. It was then that he first whispered his idea to me.

"Do you want to go to an island full of bars for the summer? Do you want to go to Put-In-Bay and work with me?" he asked. His eyes had a twinkle as he wiped his face with my shirt.

"What? Don't give me that look! Your shirt isn't clean; you haven't bathed in a month! Andi, he won't find you there. Javi will never know to look for you at Put-In-Bay."

I gasped and began weeping again. I hadn't heard that name spoken in over a month.

"Come on. It will be fun. What are you going to do here all summer with Charlie and Becky?" He started laughing, repeating my parent's names. I actually started laughing with him. I began thinking, *Yeah, I could do this!*

Put-in-Bay, in case you are confused, reader, is an island full of bars on Lake Erie. That's just what every depressed, very confused nineteen-year-old needs, right?

This is a scary chapter for me. There's lots of stuff I wish I could erase from this next phase of my life. Or, do I? I walked through fire, and God carried me out in one piece. But, my vision board does say, "Today is the day I write MY own story." So, here it goes.

Driving up to Catawba to put my car on the ferry to reach the island, I began to feel better. I was excited to see the barge that would be taking me over to all that awaited me at P.I.B. Now smiling and thinking about my new home for the next four months, I once again felt hopeful of the new life I would begin.

Once on the ferry, I forgot about New Jersey–for at least five minutes. "Andi, you are too skinny; we are going to have to work on fattening you up this summer. For crying out loud, your hip bones are sticking out! When is the last time you have eaten anything?" Daren asked me, as he pulled up my shirt to check out my stomach. Shooing his hand away, we chugged down our Sun Country Wine Coolers in paper cups, filled from the two liters that were hidden as stowaways.

"Who needs food when you have booze? Hey, I hear the Lonz Winery is outstanding. Remind me when we unpack to go and get a schedule of the winery's hours," I said to him as we looked out over the water, bouncing with the ferry as it dipped and splashed with the wake of boats passing us in the opposite direction.

Thinking how nice the lake air felt on my face, I was happy with myself. I had not cried in three days. Just then, a guy came up to me and leaned with me over the side of the boat. He said, "*Hey.*" A whistle blew from the top of the ferry, signaling we were almost on land. At that very moment, I thought, *Great, here we go with these Midwest boys. He would not make it in New York for one damn minute.*

I didn't even respond. I just turned my head and moved my sunglasses down my nose to make eye contact with Daren. He took one look at my expression and was at my side in a millisecond.

"Is that your car?" the guy asked, pointing to my car. I still didn't say a word as I stared off at the water, pretending he wasn't even there.

My heart had a scar. Well, it was actually more like my heart had a coat of armor. Knock, knock? (*Echo.*) Nope, no feelings whatsoever in there. This was especially true for feelings that involved love or guys. I was not going to allow any more pain. I swore to myself, *No more men until I get my shit together.*

"I heard your stereo," he continued, "I love the Violent Femmes. I saw them in concert last summer. Which is your favorite song?" The guy was smiling a big, toothy grin. All I could think was, *Huh? I wonder where this kid is from.*

I forgot to mention, at this point, I pretty much only wore black clothes with red lipstick. And, I started smoking–a lot. I also listened to alternative music only.

"I like 'Blister in the Sun,'" I said, staring off at the shore that was about five minutes away.

"Oh, man, that is a great one! I don't remember too much of the concert, though. I was so wasted and pretty high," he said as he looked at the shore with me, smiling and shielding his eyes from the setting sun.

Deciding to play along–I didn't want to be known as an ice queen the minute I docked–I asked him, "Where are you from anyways? Did I catch an accent?" I knew it was definitely different than anything I had heard around here.

"Wow, yes! Very good. I am from Canada," he said, holding his hand out. "My name is Justin." Even though it was extremely awkward, I did not move or extend my hand.

"Her name is 'Not Interested'! Thank you very much!" Daren piped up, now standing between us with his arms folded. He had permed his hair and colored it orange the day before we left. He looked like he was trying to become a member of the Thompson Twins or A Flock of Seagulls.

"Oh, hey man. Justin." He held his hand out, which Daren shook like he was jacking up a tire on my car. Daren put his hand on Justin's shoulder and started explaining to him we were sharing a room together in the dorms.

I didn't care. I let Daren ramble on. This guy knew there was not a chance in hell we were *together*. But, what I liked about Justin was that he said he was high at the concert, and he sat and listened politely to Daren.

The horn started blowing at the top of the ferry, which made everyone leave the deck and head over to the cars to be ready to drive off the boat when we docked.

Instead of getting ready to drive, I was thinking to myself, *Damn it, Christine. Go get it! Go get the t-shirt!* As Daren escorted his new friend to my car and poured him a paper cup full of wine cooler from the two-liter, I went to the back of my car and raised my hatch. I grabbed Javi's t-shirt out of my pillowcase and stormed off to the edge of the ferry.

"Hey, lady, get in your car!" The boat master was now screaming and telling me I couldn't go to the edge of the boat. So I walked to the back of the boat and pretended I couldn't hear him.

Standing at the back of the ferry, I threw his shirt up. The air caught it and threw it right into the churning current, taking it into the dark water and drowning it within seconds.

"Let me go! Do you hear me? Let. Me. Go!" I screamed at the wind, pointing up to the sky. I was hoping somehow the wind would carry my words. As I closed my eyes, I wished they would swirl through the air until they found their way to his doorstep.

Holding on to the edge of the boat, I was so pissed at myself that I actually started laughing. I stood there, mad as hell, but I actually started dancing. I was kind of moonwalking, thinking, *At least you are hearing music, Christine!*

I threw my hands up in the air and screamed at the top of my lungs, *"YES! YES! YES!"* I bounced on the back of the boat and shook my bum, screaming,*"GOOD-BYE!"*

I went over to my car with a new skip in my step. I did not feel heavy anymore. Even though, if I lost much more weight, I am pretty sure I would have been hospitalized. All bets were off. I started partying like I was testing my liver on an hourly basis.

If you were messed up, you were my new best friend. If you said you were a druggie teen runaway, then you and I were surely going to hang out–the weirder the better. My thoughts ran along these lines: *Did you say your name was Groovy? Awesome! Smoke pot at eleven am? Hand it over. Sure, we could get stoned together. No problem. Did you say party on a boat?*

What time are you leaving the dock? And what beverages will you be serving? Partying and having a good time was all I cared about.

I was everyone's friend. When I walked into a party, the crowd would raise their glasses shouting, "Christine!" I paid for rounds of drinks and would dance until the wee hours of the night, closing down the bar. Not one person, besides Daren, knew the *real* Christine.

All anyone knew about me was that I loved to party–a lot. I was the girl who would cliff dive at midnight and climb the lighthouse at two am or sneak on a stranger's boat to sit on the deck and drink his beer. I had almost managed to get through the entire summer without allowing one single person to get close to my heart. I was proud of this–not to mention, I was drunk all the time.

Then there was one night when I confessed to Justin every deep, dark secret I had been holding in. We were sitting up on the lighthouse deck. Blackouts had become regular with me, so the next day, I didn't have a clue that I had told him anything. He didn't tell me right away that I had spilled the beans, so to speak. He waited to tell me.

We saved each other. Justin came knocking on my door one Sunday. "Hey, Christine, are you up?" He gently opened my door, swore at the door as it squeaked open, and tiptoed to my bed. Leaning into my drunken body and rubbing my back, he handed me a warm cup of coffee.

Rubbing my eyes, I was thinking to myself, *I must still be drunk?*

"Hey, Justin. What time is it?" I paused and then asked him, "Actually, what *day* is it?" Sitting up, my nose finally noticed the beautiful aroma of coffee.

"It is Sunday. I was wondering if you wanted to go over to the mainland with me today," he said as he pulled the covers off me. Ordering me to go shower, he said we had forty-five minutes before the next ferry left.

"Where are we going?" I asked him in a whispered tone. I was already thinking, *Hey, there is a bar on the mainland that I hear has the best bloody marys and pizza.*

He leaned in and said one word that I will never forget: church. He was now over in my closet, throwing clothes all over. All I could think was, *What in the heck? Church?*

The ride on the ferry to the mainland was quiet. Neither one of us really spoke. I just kept thinking, *Church? Okay, this will be one thing I haven't tried in years.* You see, I grew up in a house with no religion.

Well, once in a while, I would go to church with my Grandma Rose. She would tell me, "Chrissie, please go to church with Grandma tomorrow; it would make Grandma so happy." I would go because I loved her, and I loved to please her. However, I usually sat there feeling lost.

My father had grown up in the Catholic school system and had religion at his door on a daily basis. My mother, well, I don't know. She really never talked about her opinion on God. Her idea of talking about God was only to tell us how awful the Catholic Church was. This was all very confusing as a kid. I mean, we would pray before each meal at the dinner table. We knew who Jesus was, but his story was never *really* explained to us.

Now, before I move on, reader, I must offer some advice. If you have never heard a gospel choir perform, run–do not walk–to the nearest performance. Please, dear reader, put it on your bucket list. Even better, put it on your vision board. It will be one of the most moving things you will ever experience. No matter where you are at the moment spiritually, I can promise you one thing: you will hear God, and He will resonate with you.

The ground shook outside the little church as we pulled into the parking lot, which was tucked away on a dead-end street. I remember looking at my reflection in the mirror of the visor on the passenger side. I did not recognize my own reflection anymore. I looked so tired.

"Come on! Hurry; the service has started," Justin said as he came around to my car door and opened it. I can remember feeling softened and taken back by his chivalry. Without thinking twice, he took my hand and wrapped his fingers tightly around mine.

We climbed the narrow, cracked concrete stairs. I remember feeling very anxious, Christmas-morning anxious, like when I was a little kid waiting to open gifts.

We opened the front doors; people were standing with their arms in the air, and music floated in every corner. Singing, clapping, smiling, and crying, the crowd was decorated by the colorful explosions of rainbow prisms that floated in the air from the enormous stained glass windows that ran floor to ceiling in the back of the church. It was almost like the beauty of the windows was celebrating in the noon sun with us.

"Let The River Run" was coming to a vibrant, uplifting crescendo. I didn't know what was going on with me. I was standing there, hearing these people sing, watching them moving, clapping, and holding palms up to sky. It was breathtaking! I felt like I was walking in a dream.

Justin looked over at me and smiled with every muscle in his face. He said through his tears, which skipped down his face, "Christine, it's not too late for us."

Everyone in the room was singing:

Oh, My heart is aching,
We're coming to the edge,
Running on the water,
Coming through the fog,
Your sons and daughters.
It's asking for the taking,
Trembling shaking,
Oh, my heart is aching.
Let all the dreamers
Wake the nation.
Come, the new Jerusalem.

Building their voices together, singing in complete unison, swaying together, and holding hands, they were beautiful. A stranger reached over to me and grabbed my hand and held it high.

I swallowed deep, as I could feel one tiny little ember pierce through my protective armor, the shield I had tightly wrapped around my beating, broken heart. I did not understand how to penetrate that shield–until that very moment in time.

For the first time in a very long time, I did not hear my own voice saying to me, *Christine, you stupid little girl.* On this day, I cried mystical, hopeful tears and felt a new beginning.

I held my hands high in sky, smiling with people who smiled at back at me. They looked at me tenderly, with true expressions of "Welcome, child!"

All I heard this time, as I closed my eyes, was, *Hello, my brave little girl. I have been waiting for you with open arms.*

Love *Is* All You Need 13

O ne Monday, I lay on the bed watching Ed pack his bag to leave. Grabbing his pillow, squeezing it tightly, I fought back the unexpected tears that sprung to my eyes. I tried not to think of how he was leaving to go on the road once again.

I found myself thinking back to when I met Ed for the first time. Daren and I moved to Florida after our island adventure; it was always the next step in our plan. To start yet another chapter of our amazing adventures together, we wanted to work for Disney. The Mouse was our dream job. However, it was just that–a dream. The two of us moved to Florida without a job. Lord, I was so carefree back then! Who was I?

I can remember feeling homesick after the first few months of living in Florida. I would think about the way my mom made my bed and the way I would walk in the back door, into my childhood kitchen, shouting out, "Hi, Mom!" She would always stop what she was doing to come and give me her time. There was a clean house and a refrigerator full of food back at home. Even so, I did not miss their drunken parties that lasted all weekend. But, I was quickly learning that even though my parents' home was extremely dysfunctional at times, it was still my familiar dysfunction.

Working for Walt Disney World was exciting. Actually, it was amazing! However, I remember actually getting bored with Disney activities–if you can believe it. I spent the first four months of my employment exploring every inch of every park. I could have been a tour guide! I knew it all.

One day I decided to wander around on my break and watch the parade. I can remember sitting on the bench on Main Street to wait for the parade to start. I was so sad. I was dead center of the happiest place on earth, but I felt so alone and not so happy.

Then this guy walks up to me, pretty normal looking–except he did have a mullet. It was serious business in the front and party in the back. I really couldn't see his face right away. The afternoon sun backlit him from head to toe. So, I was squinting like a lunatic. Plus, I was sitting in my costume (without my name tag on). I looked like a crazy, yellow-pinstriped meringue float. There I sat, hoping the parade would bring me some cheer.

He said, "Hey, I was wondering if you could you tell me something. When does the three o'clock parade start?" He just stood there, wiping the sweat from his brow.

Sounds crazy, right? But, if you have ever worked for Disney, especially at the Magic Kingdom, you know you were asked this very question at least five times a day. Really! Tourists just could not grasp that the three o'clock parade really started at three o'clock! Hysterical.

"Three o'clock," was all I said to him. He just stood there, looking at me and grinning. I actually started to get nervous. So I said, "Really, not joking," hoping this would send him on his merry way so that I could sulk in peace.

"Does it always start at three o'clock? Hey, your shoe is untied," he said. Then he bent down, like he was actually going to tie my shoe.

I pulled my foot back and blurted out, "Yep, every day." Then I stood up and decided I would find another bench. I was thinking to myself, *Good-bye to you, you stupid tourist,* as I walked away into the crowd of people. I never once looked back at the happy, shoe-tying stranger.

That night Daren and I went to a nightclub. It was all you could drink for five dollars. So, I thought, *Why not? I ditched the parade; maybe a few beers will bring me a smile.*

I was standing at the edge of the dance floor, contemplating if I really wanted to dance to the song that was playing, when I heard a voice from behind me say, "The three o'clock parade was awesome. You should have stayed to watch it." I turned around. There was "Mr. Three O'clock Parade" (Ed). I could not believe my eyes. He smiled. I smiled. The rest was history.

I love to go down memory lane in my mind, thinking about the night I met Ed. I love remembering what I was wearing. I love how he looked at me, how he hung on my every word. Not only that, he fascinated me. Plus, he was originally from Ohio, too. That night, when the two of us learned we grew up only two hours from each other, it was magic. I was no longer homesick. I found someone who could love my home with me.

Now, I was married to him, watching him pack so his eighteen-wheeler could load up and drive him away from us. I felt the familiar doom and gloom that automatically appears. When he goes, a shadow hangs over my spirit, like it was invited.

For so many years–too many to count–I have either packed his bag or helped him pack to leave us. I try to think, *Quit your pity party; imagine what military wives feel!* Nope, it still doesn't make me feel better; it actually makes me feel worse.

I try to shake off thoughts of the dangers of being on the road. I know myself too well. If I allow my mind to drift, to think about the "what ifs" of Ed being on the road, my day will be very unproductive.

I will crawl into my comfortable, crabby shell and hide out. I'll just snap it shut, enclosing myself in my safe cocoon, only peeking my eyes out if necessary, for fear I might expose my tender underbelly to someone. Ultimately, my fear is about doing life alone. It's a fear that I have become a pro at masking from my husband–or anyone else for this matter.

"I wonder if people around this country even have a clue how hard you work to get blueberries to their supermarket!" I blurted out at him, which made him jump, not realizing I was even awake. He stopped packing and crawled across the bed to tell me good morning.

"I doubt it. But, you do. What more could I ask for?" He kissed me on my forehead and sat next to me. Looking at him in the illuminated light, I sat and smiled.

I don't see that the years have aged him. I see a young kid, the young boy who saved Christine's heart.

People always used to tell me, when our kids were younger and we were branching out to make friends in the community, "Your husband doesn't look, nor doesn't act, like a truck driver."

This comment always made me laugh until my sides hurt. I would usually respond, "Yeah, he has all his teeth, and I won't let him put naked lady mud flaps on the mini-van!" That usually made people laugh with me, but it also made them stop and realize what they just said was so stupid.

He actually looks like he could be Tony Soprano's cousin, or James Gandolfini's twin for that matter. He does *look* a little dangerous, like a possible *made man*. He could easily fit in with all the Italian mafioso stereotypes that movies often portray. But, that is just his shell. Our daughter actually tells him he looks like a giant panda with a frown.

Ed has the kindest eyes. He is so shy and quiet–and is very okay with being quiet–especially around others. I, on the other hand, *well.* You have been reading about me. You know by now that I am not quiet or shy.

I never really got the whole *yin-yang* thing until I met Ed. Thinking back to when we were dating, we were so young that it never drove me crazy that he didn't want to dance with me. He would sit and watch me as I twirled and danced all over the dance floor.

Holding my beer, my purse, and handfuls of napkins, he would wait for me to blow over to the table and knock all kinds of stuff everywhere. He was ready to wipe up the mess I created with his napkins. Or he would wipe my sweaty brow for me when I took dancing intermissions to come over and kiss him. We are totally Oscar and Felix from *The Odd Couple*. *Note to self: Take Ed dancing. He deserves some fun; plus, I love the way he looks at me when I dance.*

I will never forget that at one of Eddie's baseball games a mom said to me, "Good Lord, Christine, your husband, he wears quite the murderer stare! What on earth is he thinking about?" I didn't have the energy to explain to her, "Celeste, that's just a long line of Italian heritage standing right there. That look is simply part of his DNA."

I had a hard time not laughing out loud when I looked over at him. Ed stood with feet firmly planted, scowling furiously, looking out at the baseball diamond, and watching our son round third base to steal home and score for the team. He stood with his arms folded, not speaking a word. The energy that surrounded him was clear. *Back off!* He had this look like he was hoping his *guys* had finally found a place to bury the body so that he could go home and eat a bowl of pasta in peace.

As I watched him, I knew he was focused on the beauty of his athletic son. I knew our son's baseball games helped Ed think about home when he was gone. They were his movie freeze frames that he tucked in his mind to make the long, winding roads bearable. Ed was always all in with our son and his sports. I believe those games, those moments of being a proud dad, helped keep us in his heart when he was away for weeks at a time.

I told Celeste, "Watch this." Then I yelled over to Ed, "Ed, hey darlin', do you want a Gatorade?" I smiled and held up a cold beverage. He turned and looked at me; his whole face changed. His stone demeanor completely melted. He went from a scary mobster to this sweet, humble man. He shrugged his shoulders and put his hand out, smiling at me.

"You can read my mind!" He walked over, kissed me on the cheek, and took the drink from my hands. Then he leaned down and said, "Hello, Celeste," smiling with his kind eyes and genuine, peaceful grin.

She started giggling like a schoolgirl and was practically twirling her bubble gum, looking up at him from her folding chair. I just smiled at her and winked–not that it was important for anyone to understand Ed but me. Believe me; my husband can take care of himself. I just wanted people to see what I saw, since people didn't get to see much of him. Ever.

Focusing back on Ed packing, I watched him folding up his t-shirts. "Well, I will tell you one thing. I refuse to eat a single *blue* anything anymore!" I said to him. I buried my head into the pillow, telling myself to think about the mammogram that was awaiting me in less than three hours.

Focus on that machine trying to rip your boob from your chest wall, I kept telling myself, hoping the scenario I painted in my head would take my mind off him packing.

I hate crying on him when he is moments from leaving us. But, it was too late. He knows my anger is only going to bubble out, cresting when I tell him please to find another job. But, like his Italian heritage, being a truck driver was passed down to him from four generations.

"Hey, come on now. You already won't eat watermelon, kiwi, or strawberries. Now you are going to get pissed at blueberries, too?" he asked as he leaned in, laughing and resting his forehead on mine.

He knows that the foods that take him away from me do bring us money. But, I wonder if anyone out there knows that Ed's lack of sleep is taking years off his life–just to get a watermelon to the Fourth of July party? Oh, well, I let all that go, and I threw my hands around his neck.

"Well, I will never, ever forgive watermelons. Ever! You missed the birth of our son to deliver that load to Buffalo–in case you forgot," I said to him, reburying my head in the heap of covers. But I was thinking to myself, *Poor guy! Our son* was *two weeks early.*

Trying to fend off my hot-lava anger that easily erupts when I think about how scared I was that day, delivering Eddie all alone, I decided not to mention produce anymore. Instead, I started planting kisses all over his face and singing "Rocket Man" to him (totally out of key).

"No, I didn't forget. Okay, fine, you can hate watermelon. But, you love blueberry pancakes. You better re-think tossing blueberries from your 'I-love-them list,'" he said as he paused, kissing my hand and scooting off the side of the bed to finish packing.

He used to laugh at me when I first met him. I used to have these "lists" that I kept about everything. Lists of things I loved. Lists of things I really loved. Things I kind of loved. Things I wasn't sure about loving yet but was giving a try, to see if they might make any of my existing lists of love.

I know, right? What in the world, Christine? But, remember, I was working for Disney when I met Ed. Thinking about love and all the happily-ever-after crap came naturally.

On our fifth date, he brought me three different kinds of flowers because he couldn't remember which flower was on which list. He told me that night he knew it was all good and that my lists were very confusing, but they all involved me loving things. Then he kissed me, and he asked me if he could be on one of my lists.

"Hey, Ed, when you get back home, maybe I could sit down and read you my book. You know, what I have written so far. I mean, if you want too," I said, thinking, *Christine, eventually he will have to read Chapter Eleven. Rip off the band aid! Your scars need to be aired out, or your heart will never truly heal.*

"Sure, sounds good. Why did you stop reading it to me?" he asked as he zipped up his duffle bag and flipped on the bedside light. Now he was making direct eye contact with me.

"No special reason. I just took a little longer on the last few chapters. That's all. I just want to keep you in the loop, so when Ellen turns to you and says, 'Ed, your wife is quite the author,' you know what she is talking about." I started laughing. He knows that, to me, attaining best-selling-author status and being on *The Ellen DeGeneres Show* go hand in hand.

"Is it about your childhood? Is that why you have been playing angry rap around here for days?" he asked, giving me a sideways glance as he looked through his wallet.

"It's not angry. They are powerful words that just sound angry," I protested, knowing Eminem is a tad angry. But, I have to be honest; I love Marshall (Eminem) Mathers.

Another weird side tip about me: I think Eminem is a true poet. To look at me, I don't think one person would have a clue I like his music. I do believe that's partly why I love his music; it's my secret. Well, it was until now.

His music helped me as I pulled up all that long-lost confusion, heartbreak, and anger following the "Javi" chapter. And, music has always been able to sway my moods. I think that is because of my true love of words. Heaven. It's double Heaven when you mash the two together in the form of musical poetry.

Reader, download "Lighters" by Eminem, featuring Bruno Mars. Get the unedited version–but only if your ears can hear the song, ignore the curse words, and listen to the true meaning behind it. Trust me. If you are having a *day*, this song will help.

"No, it's not really a ton of childhood stuff, mostly my teen years and up. I need to become a best selling author first! Then I can go deeper with book number two," I said to him as I started giggling and threw my pillow at him. We have talked in the dark late at night about me being a successful author and making that my new career. He is my number one fan, or so he tells me now. He promises he will move every book off of every endcap at every bookstore in town if my book isn't already displayed there for everyone to see.

"Okay, sounds good. I'm looking forward to it. Do you want to go tag team the garbage and take it down before the garbage men come around the corner?" he asked, pulling my covers off of me.

I hate Mondays because it is trash day, and that means dragging the mounds of garbage down to the curb. I began teasing Ed that our three-legged, pregnant raccoon might be lurking in the shadows–and she doesn't part with her cans very easily.

"Don't tell me that! You know that thing scares me!" His voice trailed off, but then he blurted out, "Hey, don't you have your mammogram today?" He rubbed his forehead with a worried look. I was not really sure if he was thinking about the huge raccoon that could possibly bite him or my mammogram. I found myself thinking, as we went to get the garbage, *What Freudian thing was that about? How did he get from raccoons to remembering my mammogram? Totally hysterical!*

He was starting to get frustrated that four people could make so much garbage. To lighten his mood a little, I teased him, thinking, *Lord knows this guy could laugh more! Heck, we both could.*

"Yep, I heard the imaging center has this new Boob Masher 3000, or is it 4000? State of the art–that's all I know. I hear the machine spits out tissues as your eyes water from the shear agony of this new machine as it tries to photograph your numb boob! Did you know they squeeze your boob like they are trying to make enough lemonade for hundreds of people? Doesn't that sound awesome?" I shouted to him as I drug a garbage can with all my might up the incline at the end of the driveway.

I did not realize that my voice was echoing off the garage door. So, every neighbor in a five-mile radius probably heard all about my boob as they sat down to eat their Eggos.

He stood there grinning. Then he shook his head and walked over to me. Taking me in his arms, he engulfed me with his enormous, safe, comfortable hug.

"Well, I am sure if you have anything to do with it, you will start a petition to boycott all lemonade within a hundred miles. All the people you know better watch out with you." I started laughing. Even though I was using my infamous humor to deflect the serious stuff, he wasn't smiling anymore, and he was quiet.

The lump I have felt in my left breast for several weeks now was definitely part of the serious stuff. The toxic worry I had been keeping all to myself needed to stay inside, unspoken. There was no way was I going to share this with him now. He needed to leave with peace of mind, not worry.

I watched him drive down the road. He paused under the street light two houses down from our driveway. So I waved to him, thinking that he was probably waving. Going into the house, I contemplated rescheduling my mammogram. I tried to think of an excuse to tell the doctor I work for, but I said to myself, *No excuses, Christine. Cut the crap!*

"Hey, doc, I can't have my mammogram today because. . ." Nope, he would see through anything. He is *the* best Oncologist in the state of Florida, for so many different reasons. He would escort me over there if he had too. Besides, the women I care for every day with breast cancer are my unsung heroes. I could never hold back my shameful tears if I bailed on my mammogram.

The problem was that I knew something was wrong. I just felt it. Going over to my cell phone, I picked it up. Huh? I had a text from Ed.

That's why he paused under the streetlight, to type this to me! His text said, "Do not cancel this appointment, Christine! I mean it! Xo"

Hmmm. I am that *transparent?*

UNICORN 14

The girl behind the desk at the imaging center greeted me with a sunny grin.

"Hey, Christine. Good morning! Sign in over here, and we will get you right in. Gosh, Christine, I can't believe it has been six months since your last mammogram! Are you working today?" Debbie asked as she looked at a patient holding his stomach behind me.

I used to work over at the hospital with Debbie. It's good to see us both growing and evolving in the career world as we deal with growing teens. I have known Debbie since, well, it seems like forever. Our kids grew up together. I will never forget that her son threw up root beer floats all over my family room sofa.

"Hey, Debbie. Yep, I work in an hour," I said to her as I looked at my phone to gage how late I will probably be. "Do you think I will make it out of here in time?" I was wondering whether to text the doctor I work for and give him the heads up that I would be late.

As I looked around the packed waiting room, I knew "late" would turn into a half day off. I started shivering with worry as I signed my name on the form to check in. This was the price to pay for knowing so many people in this town; at least two people I know very well would see my naked boobs in about thirty minutes. The same two people that I would, no doubt, run into at the deli counter at the grocery store the next day.

However, I love walking around the campus of this hospital. And knowing so many different people makes me smile. There are so many brilliant minds working here–too many to count, actually. From the janitor to the dishwasher to the PBX operator and the faithful volunteers–even the number one surgeon. Each person at this hospital has something new to add to my day. I love it. It may sound corny, but people fascinate me just as much as words. So many heroic people here doing daily good deeds often leaves me speechless.

Debbie leaned over the counter and said to me quietly, "I dunno about that, but we will try. We will do our best–since you do work for 'The Man,'" she said as she smiled and winked at me. I felt proud because the doctor I work for is amazing. He never believes me when I share with him all the nice things people say about him.

I can never figure out why he doesn't understand he is like a 1967 Shelby GT500. You know, Eleanor from *Gone in Sixty Seconds*? It may sound like a weird comparison, but for crying out loud, he is an oncologist. He is a unicorn, just like Eleanor.

As I found a seat in the waiting room, my mind started thinking about American-made muscle cars: the duel exhaust, speed, lowered suspension, cobra rims. I actually started laughing out loud, remembering I was a weird little girl. I asked for race tracks every year for Christmas. I had a thing for matchbox cars, too.

I don't think the doctor truly realizes how many people I really do know in this town. You know, now that I think about it, amazing seems too trite to describe his medical mind. Sure, after he leaves the office, he is probably a regular guy, with regular problems, putting his pants on one leg at a time, just like the rest of us. But, God has graced him with a gift. He has the ability to understand cancer and the drugs that will possibly save a persons life. He knows how to destroy this cancer that lives inside of them. It's unreal in my eyes. Anyone who makes a career waging the war against cancer is a unicorn.

Some days, I just stare at him while his mind is calculating combinations of medicines that will destroy a tumor. This usually makes him say to me, "Yes, Christine?" Thank heavens he uses a very kind voice, because I know sometimes I don't realize I am just staring. I usually throw all my jumbled words out in the air, asking him a question about something I have been thinking about. He doesn't mind, though. He is always willing to teach me something.

I think I realized the day I met him that his office was going to be my new home. I knew he was a very humble genius. Really, if I had his degrees and knowledge, Lord! I would probably remind everyone, every five minutes. "Hello, yes, I am an oncologist." Not him, though. He is so relatable to so many people, on so many levels.

Plus, his patient care is unbelievable. His mother must have loved him well; that is all I can think of. You can't learn in medical school how to treat someone as a priceless individual. Some doctors just have it, beside manner, while other doctors don't have a clue how treat a patient. Some doctors stand and stare at you, like you could be a grilled cheese sandwich for all they care! Not the doctor I work for. I like to pride myself on working for a doctor who raises the bar on a daily basis.

In the waiting room, I got lost in my thoughts: *Hmmm. Note to self: ask him if he minored in psychology. Lord, he is my age? When did he go to college? When he was, what, twelve years old?*

"Christine, you can come back now." I glanced over to the voice now calling my name. Yep, as I predicted, it was Tracy, a long time P.T.A. mom who volunteered with me for ages. She was grinning at me, holding her arms out to give me a hug as I walked towards her. I started to sweat, realizing I couldn't remember if I shaved my armpits. *Damn, why did I rush this morning? Oh, shake it off, Malone; think about that lump. Focus.*

"Hey! I haven't seen you in ages," I said to her as I leaned in and gave her a big squeeze.

"Come in here; let's get you in a gown," Tracy said as she took my hand and led me to the locker room for patients. I went behind the little stall and started to undress while she stood on the other side. She started telling me all about her kids and how she still volunteers at the middle school. She said she drives by my house almost everyday and thinks about stopping by to chat. All I could think was that her idle chatter was making me forget about my worry. I realized that all I had said to her in reply was, "Oh, my… yeah, that's great." As I tried to comfort my skittish mind, I decided that this could be a perk of knowing so many people. If she does see an ominous lump, I can probably get her to tell me what she sees.

Standing in horrifying positions as the machine squeezed my breast in various poses, I saw the blob on the screen when I looked over. Tracy saw it too. Then she saw my face, and all chitchat came to a screeching halt. She released my breast from the torture chamber and asked me to please sit down. She left the room, not able to make eye contact with me anymore. A different woman came in and asked me to follow her to another room. The doctor had asked the new tech to escort me into a different, freezing ice chamber; he wanted me to wait and have an ultrasound.

My mind immediately started racing. I tried to tell myself, *It's a good thing. You know, Christine, this is just a closer look.* As I lay on the table and waited for the ultrasound tech to come in, I stared at the ceiling. I felt completely numb because I knew what I saw. The tech took twenty different pictures without uttering one single word. I turned my head as tears filled my eyes.

I was trying to stay sane. *Just breathe, Christine.* This was my mantra, and I played it over and over in my mind. I spend my days with cancer, and all my knowledge was stuck in my throat, a big lump of silent worry. I didn't even reach up to wipe my tears; I just kept my head turned to the side, because they wouldn't stop flowing down my cheeks.

I heard the doctor come in; I felt him standing next to me, but I still didn't turn my head to look at him. I was all by myself, and I didn't want to see the anything *yet.*

The doctor said to me over his shoulder, as he stood at the machine in between us, "Christine, we took lots of pictures. I will look them over, and we will go from there. Okay, Christine?"

"Sure, no problem. Thank you. Can I get dressed now?" I asked him as I held my scrubs in my hands on top of me. I still didn't turn my head to look at him. Sitting up quickly, I kept my back to him.

"Yes, of course. Are you working today?" he asked me. I could feel him standing behind me. However, I didn't turn around. I just sat there staring at the light switch on the wall.

"Yep, I sure am. If you need me, I will be there," I said to him as I used my shoulder to wipe my tears away. I took in a silent, deep breath. I didn't realize I was holding my breath until I heard the door close behind me.

I got dressed in less than twenty seconds, exiting the room quickly; I smiled to everyone on my way out, not once showing a soul the worry that plagued me. I made my rounds, giving hugs, thanking everyone, and telling Tracy to keep in touch.

Walking back over to my office, I decided to hold my left breast gently in my hand. I was not worried that someone would see me or stare at my oddness. My breast was screaming mad at me! Cradling it was all I could do to apologize properly for that mashing pain! All I could think was, *This sun feels wonderful on my face!*

As I walked across the parking lot to my building, I looked up to the bright blue sky and threw a kiss up. I hoped my Claudia would feel her morning kiss from me.

I thought about how much I missed her. My sweet Claudia had, indeed, passed away. I wondered if I would ever be able to eat anything with pumpkin again. *Silly girl, of course you will.* It was as if I could hear her now in my mind. *Christine, I died. But, I have not left you! Eat pumpkin and live!*

I decided to look up at the sky in the parking lot. With my arms open wide, I threw my head back, smiled, and shouted, "Thank you, God!" This outburst sent about fifteen birds flying from the bushes next to me. I said to them, "Go on, little birdies. Take my words to God and Claudia."

Grinning as the elevator took me up to my office, I was excited to see all my patients. I love Mondays at work. As I help each patient who walks through our door, I celebrate with them, rejoicing in the triumphs of the little things they got to experience again over the weekend–triumphs like tasting ice cream again instead of metal or getting two hours of sleep instead of only fifteen minutes. I reminded myself, *It is the little things, Christine.*

"Good morning, everyone!" I sung to all our patients sitting in the waiting room. I have blown through this office door for almost eighteen months; each time, I feel happy and loved. Walking through this door every day brings me purpose, blessings, and hope. It makes me smile just thinking about it.

"Hey, girl. Did you have a great weekend?" I asked my coworker as I sat at my desk, still holding my boob. Putting an enormous piece of gum in my mouth, I hoped I didn't make everyone sick over at the imaging center with my terrible coffee breath. I sat and smiled at my coworker as I twirled in my new swivel chair and listened to her talk on the phone.

"Good morning! Yeah, my weekend was okay–a little on the boring side, though. Hey, the doctor wants to see you in his office. He has called up here three times, asking if you were here yet," she said as she pointed to the phone with her ink pen, signaling to me to look. He was actually on the intercom again.

Picking up the phone, I cleared my throat and said, a little too cheerfully, "Good morning! How are you this morning? Did you have a nice time in Montréal for your conference?" I held my gum in my fingers, for fear I would chomp too loudly.

"Good morning, Christine. (He paused for a little too long.) Yes, thank you, it was okay, very cold. Christine, when you get settled, could you please come back to my office? Okay? Thank you, Christine."

He hung up. Uh, oh, he said my name too much in one sentence. I thought to myself, *Well, his tone was okay. I don't think I have ticked him off about something. Hmmm, I wonder what this is about?*

Telling my coworker I would be right back, I picked up my notebook and pen. I stopped and said hello to a few patients the nurses were taking back to exam rooms. Realizing my breast did not hurt anymore, I felt happy. I started humming leftover songs that were floating around in my mind.

Going to the door of his office, I saw him leaning over his computer, looking at something very intently. He didn't see me standing there.

He looked up as I gently tapped on his door. He came from around his desk, asking me to sit down. Wait a minute. I knew this look! This is the look he gives our patients when he delivers bad news. It's his much-softened, caring look. He gives steady eye contact that is not threatening, but poignant. I have studied his mannerisms and facial expressions to help me reach patients on a comfort level, like only he can. My mind started screaming; thank God the doctor couldn't hear it!

Please don't say what I think you are going to say! Please…please…God. Am I ready to ride the cancer coaster? I bowed my head, for fear I would embarrass myself and start weeping like a baby.

"Christine, the mass in your left breast has doubled in size since your last mammogram six months ago." He sat down next to me and placed a soft hand on one of my shoulders. I pulled my gum out of my mouth for fear I would accidentally swallow it and choke. My eyes began to sting from the crocodile tears that hung on my eyelids.

"I am not saying it is anything yet, Christine. Let's get it out first. We'll see what it is and go from there. Okay, Christine?" His voice dropped to almost a lullaby kind of tone as he said my name.

I realized my tears were dripping onto my notebook, making my notes from yesterday unreadable. I clutched my notebook as if it was my treasured baby blanket from long ago. I just sat there sniffing, nodding my head, and wishing Ed was home so he could hug me tightly when nightfall comes. I still didn't speak, nor did he. He just let me have my moment.

"Okay." That's it; that's all I could say. As hard as this whole thing was to swallow, I still felt like the luckiest girl alive. Cancer or not, I believed God led me to this office to be cared for by this doctor and these nurses. How else could I ever make heads or tails of my journey thus far?

"I would like the surgeon to operate next Wednesday, Christine, if that's okay," the doctor said as he slowly stood, keeping his palm on my shoulder.

"Christine, it will all be okay. Okay?" My waterworks instantly shut off. Why? Because, my heart believed him. This is something very rare for me; typically, I believe no one.

Deciding to leave the room, I turned to him and said a soft thank you. The doctor was now back at his desk, looking at his computer screen. He stopped, looked up, smiled, and said, just as softly, "You are welcome, Christine."

Finding my way to the bathroom, I got wet paper towels to put on my cheeks. You see, I puff up like a puffer fish when I cry. I become a red, swollen, spiky mess! I didn't want my patients to see me crying.

My co-worker had her arms out to hug me before I could even make it to the bathroom. I stopped and embraced her, thinking, *I love her hugs.*

She took my hand and guided me into the kitchen, twirling me around so that I stood before our wall of canvas hearts. I started thinking to myself, *Wow! Is she going to tell me she will paint my heart for me in case I die? Good lord, what is going on?* I looked over to see her smiling. Her radiant smile could light a dark forest for miles; she is absolutely beautiful, inside and out.

"Christine, I feel your tears. I am so sorry you have to start your day being so sad," she said as she started hugging me again, grinning from ear to ear.

"Its okay. I don't think it has sunk in yet. I am afraid it might take a few days," I said to her as I rubbed my eyes with my fists. Scratching them, I made them feel like hot sandpaper. Worried my contacts would fly out of my eyes, I covered my eyes with both my hands.

"You know how much he loved you. Just think how happy Sam is in Heaven right now. Christine, he is with our Lord, pain free," she said, squeezing my hand and looking tenderly at the wall of hearts.

However, it was like someone took the biggest icicle that could possible hang after an ice storm and drove it through my heart. I actually started gasping, trying to catch my breath. Pulling away from her hug, I went over and sat down on the little chair at the table. I could not breathe. I looked around, and thought, *Oh, my God, please! No, no, no. Sam died?*

Now, I put my face in my hands and really started sobbing the movie heroine kind of sobs. I just kept saying, "I didn't know. I didn't know. When did he die?" She was now rubbing my back, saying, "Shhhhhh," so gently. I looked up, and she was crying too.

"Christine, I am sorry. I thought that's why you were crying when you came out of the doctor's office. Oh, dear, sweetie, I am so sorry." She took my hand and sat down next to me. "Please, sweetie, look at me. Why were you crying?" she asked me with a very sincere look. I swear somehow the two of us are related. We just haven't figured out how yet. Our hearts are always in synch with each other; it's amazing.

I looked in her direction, but kept my snot-covered face hidden with my hands.

"My heart is broken. Sam died? When did he die?" I asked as I thought to myself, *Crying makes me vomit, and that's something my co-workers don't know about yet.*

Sam was my NYPD angel. We bonded instantly. Who am I kidding? I "bond" with every patient. However, I only let a select few in to see the real Christine. And Sam, he naturally glided into my heart. He called me his bluebird. He chose *blue* because of my eyes and *bird* because I flew into his heart.

"No way, Christine, you first. Tell me this instant why you are crying." She was bending her face up underneath my chin as if to tell me, *I am not going anywhere.* She tried to pull my hands away from my face; she kept saying my name.

"I have a lump in my left breast; it has grown, doubled in size! I am getting it taken out next Wednesday. I thought you brought me back here to tell me you would paint my heart for me, in case I died." I actually surprised myself and started giggling as I blew a few snot bubbles, laughing at my whole morning!

"Oh, my goodness! My sweet friend, I am so sorry!" She started laughing with me and put her arms on top of me.

"I am so sorry, but I've got to be honest. God forbid, but if something were to happen to you, I wouldn't just paint a little heart on the wall. This whole room would be painted in rainbow! Actually, I would paint the whole building in rainbow with my bare hands for you."

She fell silent, laid her head gently on my folded arms, and said in a hushed tone, "Trust in God's plans for you." We just hung out for a few more minutes, soaking up the promise of God's love–until my stomach could no longer hold the acidic tears and snot I had been swallowing.

"I have to go to the bathroom," I said as I pulled away from her loving embrace. I knew I was going to throw up soon—maybe even before I could leave the room. She pulled my hands closer to her and tucked a card in the pocket of my scrubs.

"Here. Before you leave, Sam's wife brought us all cards this morning." Before she let me go, she squeezed my hand and smiled at me.

After throwing up nothing but acid, I decided to lie on the bathroom floor on my back. I kept wondering how I was really going to react to all this news I just got. I know what you are thinking, reader. You are thinking, *Gross, Christine! The bathroom floor? Disgusting!* But, you have to understand. The women I work with are spotless, and our employee-only bathroom floor was, no doubt, cleaner than my kitchen floor.

As I lay there, listening to my breathing, with mounds of cold, wet paper towels teetering on my face, I thought about my life, my journey, and my climb. I thought about my kids, my husband, my parents, my siblings, my nieces and nephews. I also thought about my coworkers, Daren, my friends, my patients, and all of my extended family too. The doctor I worked for, my dogs, and Claudia and Sam were all in my thoughts. The mysterious lump that was now invading my left breast, uninvited, was making me feel blessed in some weird way. I didn't think of any bucket list or the things I had yet to do. Instead, I thought of all the things I had and the people who loved me. I started to sing very softly to myself words I know by heart: the lyrics to "Fire and Rain" by James Taylor.

The only thing that inspired me to get off the floor that day was you. Yes, *you*, my dear reader. I have fallen in love with *you*—with just the idea of you with my book in your hands. I am humbled, and I hear music in my mind when I think of you. You, my dear reader (whomever you may be), you are my true inspiration to keep going, to write it down, and to make IT happen!

EXCUSE ME?   15

T he rest of that day I was on autopilot. I was just going through the motions. I was having a hard time with my emotions; I could not stop thinking about the mysterious lump inside of me. My mind was focused on boarding the possible chemo-cancer coaster.

It was emotional seeing my patients (my family) come through the door. These patients know me. I believe when a when a person has cancer, he acquires a new sense or is able to awaken more fully his existing senses. Truly, my patients are so aware. It makes my heart skip a beat. On several occasions, I have heard my patients say exactly what was on my mind.

"Christine, come over here right now," my patient with stage-four breast cancer commanded me as she took my hand in hers.

"Yes, Ms. Rosie, what's up?" I asked, giving her a tiny smile.

"Baby, you tell me. I am feeling something very different with you today. Do you need to talk about something?" she asked as she left the bathroom with her chemo pole in tow. Moving closer to me, not waiting for my response, she hugged me. I started crying.

We have spent every weekday together for the past twelve weeks. She is one that naturally glided into my heart. Now, here I was, crying on her shoulder. *How selfish of me*, was all I could think. I could hear my mind getting angry with myself and saying, *What the heck is wrong with you, Christine?*

"Don't make me worry about you; tell me this instant, young lady!" She was following me up to the front of the office. I was trying to guide her mother-bear attitude out of earshot from anyone else.

"Just having a bad day, Ms. Rosie, that's all. Besides, you have enough on your plate without worrying about my stuff," I said as I blew my nose, looking at her through my tissue. I watched her turn beet red with anger at my comment.

"Excuse me? You let me decide what to worry about. Do you understand me? You are my Christine. You have taken care of me when I was at my weakest, at my most vulnerable time in life. Heck, you helped me change my drawers in the bathroom, didn't you?" She began to wag her finger at me, looking very cross. She put her hand on her hip and started bobbing her head.

"It's nothing. Really, I don't know if it's anything, *yet*," I said in a short tone, taking her hands in mine and shaking my head as if I hoped my brain would understand this action: *no more tears*!

"Now, look here. I don't like you like this, and you better just spit out what *it* is," she blurted out as she stood and retied my scrub ties that were hanging at my waist. She pulled me down to her and gently pushed my bangs off to the side, moving them out of my eyes, drying a few tears on my face with an already wet tissue.

"I have a lump in my left breast. It has grown. I am getting it taken out next Wednesday." Magically, I said these words with ease–not one tear fell down my face.

"Oh, my sweet child. Now, why couldn't you tell me that? What? Are you suppose to wander the earth the rest of your days without anyone caring about you? You may be a caregiver, but you can't keep this inside. Do you even remember what you told me when I was ashamed I messed my pants that day? You made me feel so much better," she said as she put both her hands on her hips, leaning forward to look up at me.

She was looking at me like a grandmother who scolds her granddaughter for eating Doritos on her white couch in the "off-limits" living room. I actually started giggling.

"Yes, I do," I said, looking down at the floor, still trying not to giggle. She told me to repeat what I told her that day and to stop *trying* her patience.

"God places people in our lives when we are at our weakest. And guess what, Ms. Rosie? I listened to God today, and he led me to you." Then I grinned at her. She grabbed my hands, and I leaned in and gave her a hug. Well, actually she pulled me to her breast and squeezed the life out of me–as if she was trying to squeeze the worry from my mind.

She whispered in my ear, as we stood hugging, "Very good, my sweet baby. This morning, Christine, God told me to pay attention to you, my sweet, tall, blue-eyed angel." Then, she pulled back from me and pointed her thumb in the direction of the doctor's office.

"You are quite the lucky little girl; you have me, God, and him (motioning with her full body to the doctor's office door again) to care for you. Baby, don't be scared. It might just be a lump. I am still here, and I had a lump. You just never know, and you will learn to be okay with not knowing. But, this is probably going to be nothing. Okay, my sweet baby?" she said as she squeezed and hugged me all over again. She ended our embrace with a hallelujah, as she clapped her hands.

Taking her back to her room with her IV pole, watching her chemo drugs swing as she walked too fast to get back to her TV, I told her, "Slow down! Judge Judy doesn't start for another twenty minutes."

Looking at her plastic IV bags full of a mysterious medicinal cocktail, I felt that cold shiver again. These were drugs that many scientists had probably given up their entire existence to create, to help save people from cancer. I let out a sigh of exhaustion and fear. It felt very empty in the valley of my heart all of a sudden.

"Hand me my blanket, sweet baby," Ms. Rosie requested, not realizing I had grabbed it on the way to her room.

"Here you go; I already have it. Let me cover you up," I said to her as her cell phone rang. She told her caller to call back her after her program.

She grabbed my hand before she hung up. I waited and listened to her while she told her caller where something was in her bathroom.

She hung up and looked up at me. "You are so tall. Get that chair over there and come sit next to me," she said, tucking her cell phone in her bra, pointing to the rolling chair over by the sink.

"Ms. Rosie, I have to get back to work. I haven't done much of anything today," I said to her, holding her hand and not moving.

"Lord, child, go get the chair, and come sit down. Don't you ever say you haven't done much today. Now, I want you to listen to me." She waited as I got the little rolling chair and sat down next to her. She started talking to me, but waved her arm out to the space in front of her, like she was also addressing an audience.

"Cancer and people. Others will share lots of stories with you, when they find out what's going on with you about this cancer. Everyone only shares the bad stuff, though. Do you hear me? It's like when you are pregnant, and everyone shares the worst possible story about her childbirth experience or a distant cousin's delivery where she almost died! Same thing. No one shares great stories about cancer or the people they know with cancer who survive." She paused, looked up at the TV, and opened her M & M's. I started bubbling with giggly laughter. She kept talking.

"You have a choice. You can decide not to listen to all that dribble and nonsense. Or, you can listen to it all. It's up to you. My advice to you: do *not* wear a noose of worry around your neck. Okay, child? Spend this next week enjoying every moment; take note of all the things that make you happy. You will never get these days back, the days before you learned the verdict about what that lump is," she said, pointing at my breast as she put more candy in her mouth. "You are going to learn a lot about yourself from this day forward. You'll learn who you really are and what you, my sweet child, are really made of. Baby, hand me the remote." She waved her little bag of candy at the counter behind me, signaling where the remote was.

I didn't even think about what came next. "Thank you for listening to God this morning, Ms. Rosie. I love you," I said to her, bowing my head. I bowed, not because I was worried I would cry, but because I was so humbled by her care for me. I felt that chill again. This time I welcomed it. I saw it as a miracle chill, sent like a lightning bolt to my heart. "Wake up, my brave little girl. Are you still there?" I heard God whispering in my ears.

"Come here. Give me another hug, and it's *Auntie* Rosie from now on! Do you hear me? And, I have always loved you, baby. Our Lord, He knows what he is doing," she said as she shooed me to move over after she hugged me; her TV program was starting. I just stood over her and smiled as she talked to the TV. I patted her hand before I left. She grabbed my fingers, squeezed them, and nodded at me.

Going to my computer, I sat at my desk and stared at the blue screen, blinking at me, waiting for me to enter my password. I began thinking about Ms. Rosie's words and how they had impacted me: *Have no worries; enjoy this week; do what you like doing, baby. You will never get these days back.* Hearing those words roll over and over in my mind, all I could think about were the things I obviously didn't know about me.

What is my favorite color? Like, really, Christine. You obviously would not have painted your house gray or decorated your family room in shades of mud if you had a favorite color, correct?

I think I like green. But, I think that only became my "favorite" color when people would say to me, "Wow, you look pretty in green!"

How do I really like my eggs? Ed asked me the other day if I wanted some scrambled eggs. To be honest, I am not sure if I even like eggs. *How do I really like my coffee?* I always tell someone, "Oh, just a little cream, if you have it." And it usually ends up burning my stomach, but I smile as I sip it from the mug, saying, "Mmm, good."

You love to tell yourself, "It will be fine!" Guess what, Christine? You never allow your heart to stumble because you are a control freak, and you fear it might not be fine!

I could hear myself screaming, *What the heck, Christine?*

Now, I do know one thing about me. I love music and chocolate. That is something I can stand by. I thought, *Lord, Christine, that isn't what your new Auntie Rosie meant! Or, was it? How can I ever tackle the big stuff if I don't even know about the little stuff with me? You just said to yourself in the elevator on the way up, 'Remember, it is about the little stuff, Christine!'*

Everything I buy at the grocery store is for someone else! What I make for dinner is never about me. Heck, do I even really like two-ply toilet paper? I don't have a clue! I buy what's on sale. I cut my own hair, for crying out loud! Why? We don't have enough money left by the time we get to me for haircuts!

Goodness sakes, I wouldn't even display an Obama sign in my yard when he ran for election because I didn't want to make waves with my Republican neighbors. These were neighbors who would always show up at my doorstep–uninvited–to share their opinions about how Obama was going to destroy this country. I just stood there and listened! *What happened to you, Christine? You love Barack! You are a Democrat and proud of that! Damn you, Christine! You have become a doormat! Oh, Lord, please tell me. How did all this happen?*

I don't even go to church anymore because it's too much hassle to get everyone out the door! I beg everyone to go to the beach. They never want to go, so we don't go! It's my favorite thing in the world, to sit in the sand, listening to the wind and watching the endless, blue sky bring in the warm waves of water.

I felt like I was possibly going to explode right there in my desk chair! Turning around, I asked my coworker, "Hey, did I hear the back door close? Did the doctor leave and go over to the hospital?" I had not realized she was on the phone until she turned around and pointed at the phone in her hands. I tapped my pen like a lunatic, waiting for her to end her phone call so she could answer me.

"Yes, he went to the hospital, but not to see patients yet. He has put a team of doctors together to look at a CD or something. He told me that if any other doctors called, I was to tell them to meet him over at radiology. Something or someone serious is on his mind today." She didn't even wait for me to respond. She picked up the ringing phone and shrugged her shoulders at me as I gave her a blank stare.

I just slumped in my chair. Her words stung my ears. *Why don't I realize how truly important I am to others? How did this happen? A team of doctors, for me?* All I could say under my breath as I shook my head was, "Amazing!" Pumped up with my new vision of ME, I went back to Rosie's room.

"Hey, Ms. Rosie, are you awake?" I said to her, leaning into the doorway and hanging onto the doorframe with one hand. I thought she was sleeping; her eyes were closed.

"Don't you mean *Auntie* Rosie? And yes, darling, I am awake." She scooted herself up in the chair and looked over to me, opening her eyes.

"Auntie Rosie," I giggled, "I forgot to tell you earlier that I love your shirt." I beamed at her with a wide smile.

She looked down and tugged at the t-shirt to straighten the smiling face that was airbrushed there—decorated in glory with a sparkly, sequined American flag.

"Of course you do, baby; that's our Barack Obama, Mr. President himself!" she said, looking down at her shirt and folding her arms around it, as if she was giving her own shirt a hug.

"I am going to take the rest of the day off. If I don't see you next week, keep me in your prayers, okay?" I said to her as I walked closer to her chair. Worrying I will block her view of the TV, I bent down and told her, "I have some stuff to figure out, Auntie Rosie." I just stood there, bent over, and gave her a full-set-of-teeth grin.

"Baby, I have been praying for you long before I even knew you. Don't you worry about me and my prayers for you. Go. Enjoy your day. Eat a big, juicy cheeseburger for me. Okay? Lord, do I miss a big cheeseburger!" she said to me, closing her eyes with a grin.

Leaving her room, I stopped and texted the doctor: "Hey, doc, can I take the rest of the afternoon off? Please?" While waiting at my desk for his response, I held my phone in my palm, looking at it like I do when I watch the lottery numbers every Saturday night on TV. I actually realized I was whispering to my phone, "Please, please, please say yes."

"Yes, of course. Please text me if you need anything," was his response. I literally jumped in the air, as if my lotto numbers had popped up.

Grabbing my purse, I stopped and wrote a sticky note for my coworker who was on the phone: "Leaving early; doctor said okay." She turned to me, grinned, and gave me the thumbs up. Thinking how much I love her happiness, I wrote her another note: "Thank you for being you." She turned to me and blew me a kiss. We waved good-bye to each other, smiling.

Waiting for the elevator at the end of the hall, I decided, *Nope! This is taking way, way too long.* I took the three flights of stairs to the parking lot, like I was in a race to get to the bottom. Sitting in my scorching hot van, I dialed Ed's number and blasted the air conditioning. He answered.

"Hey, babe. Are you driving? Do you have a quick minute to talk?" I asked him, thinking to myself, *Oh, this isn't going to be a quick minute.*

"Nope, I just stopped for lunch; I'm eating a cheeseburger. What's up?" he asked me. I know he was looking at the clock, wondering, *Why is she calling me at two in the afternoon?*

I didn't know if I should start laughing or crying. *He is eating a cheeseburger? Priceless.*

"Ed, we are going to the beach this Saturday. If you're home, I want you to go with me," I told him. I never asked for what I wanted anymore. Ever! I was going to change that.

"Sure, we could do that. How did your mammogram go?" he asked me. I could hear him sucking up his soda through a straw.

I sat in the van, not moving from the parking lot until I shared every detail of my day with him. He asked me if I wanted him to turn around and come home. In the twenty-three years I have known him, this was the first time he asked me such a question. For the first time in twenty-three years, I felt strong enough to say no–and I meant it!

SOMEWHERE OVER THE RAINBOW 16

After my parking-lot conversation with Ed, I felt drained, like I had taken a Tylenol PM and drank three wine coolers. And, it was only three in the afternoon. Visualizing a warm shower, I somehow kept my feet moving.

When I opened the front door, every light was on, the TV was on, the dryer was running, and the stereo was even on. The microwave was spinning with nothing in it. Amidst the chaos, I thought, *Well, here's a first. I am not angry with what is before me.*

Moving through the house, I turned everything off, figuring one of the kids would show themselves eventually to blame the other for this nightmare I came home too.

Deciding to pour myself a glass of wine before I headed off to the shower, I told myself, *Be careful, Christine. This is how all the boozehound housewives started in your family! It's only three in the afternoon!*

Then I heard soft little sniffles. Walking towards these sniffles, I saw Emily lying on her bed, facedown. She was fully clothed under her covers, sobbing.

"Hey, hey, what's up, Emily?" I asked in a hushed tone, sitting down next to her on her bed. When she felt me sit down, she swung her leg at me, indicating I needed to get up and get out!

I went over to her desk and sat down. I actually leaned in, looking at my reflection in her makeup mirror, which was also lit up like a Christmas tree. I shut off the light, thinking, *Later, Christine, look later.*

"Em, please tell me what's up," I said to her, trying to rub her toe, which was tapping under her covers. She pulled her foot away and screamed, "Please, Mom, leave me be!"

For some strange reason, I didn't move. This behavior yesterday would have had me at her bedside, pulling the covers off and asking, "Excuse me?" Not today. I just wanted to crawl into her bed next to her and sleep for four days.

"It's all good, Emily. I will wait until you're ready to talk," I said to her as I swirled my red wine in the glass, contemplating whether I really wanted to drink it.

"No, mother, it's not all good! Do you want to know why I am so upset? Do you?" she asked, sitting up and yelling in my direction. The static from her comforter made her hair stand out like she had touched a light bulb. I grinned at her–which was not a well-thought-out plan on my part.

"Don't you laugh at me! Do you know what I did today while you did nothing but sit at your desk? Do you? Oh, and by the way, I am never, ever going back to school! Ever!" She cocked her head to the side, opened her backpack, and threw a detention slip at me. Then she covered her entire body back up.

I unfolded the crumpled little slip of paper. I must be honest; I never thought I would see one of these fly my way with her name on it. I just sat and cleared my throat. I could not believe I was okay with not saying a word. I was actually comfortable with just sitting there. I was thinking to myself, *Well, Christine, quite a lot of firsts for you today.*

Setting my wine down on her dresser, I decided to scoot my chair to the side of her bed and wait. I looked out her window at the treetops.

"Mom, why are you just sitting there?" she shouted at me, wrestling with herself under the covers. I still didn't say a word.

"Fine! Do you know what I did today at school? Well, in first period, we had a substitute who made us watch a documentary about 9-11. It was a horrible way to start my day! Plus, I didn't feel like eating breakfast today and watching that video made my stomach burn! Then the idiot sub decided to tell us that they are still finding the remains of people who jumped that day or were blown up from the explosion of the Towers!" She blurted this out as she covered her face in her palms and shook her head.

"Oh, but wait, Mom! I had to go to the bathroom, and they did a tardy sweep, so I was locked out of my second period class. Guess what? No matter *what*, teachers do *not* open the door for you anymore, Mom! Doors always stay locked! Do you now why? Because of the Sandy Hook Elementary shooting, Mom!" she yelled. Pulling all the contents out of her backpack, she took a deep breath and continued.

"All doors stay locked every period for the whole period! No matter what! So, I had to go sit in the cafeteria and learn nothing!" she said, holding her hands up to her eyes.

I still didn't move. I think I was in shock. Then she asked me if I could "handle" more. I held my hands out, palms up, and said, "*More?*"

"Yep, more! Right before fourth period ended, the whole school was on lockdown. Do you know why? Apparently, a stupid kid brought a homemade bomb to school, and our teacher screamed at us the whole period, telling us all that she was sure one of the dumb kids around our school was going to hurt an innocent person by the end of the year. I sat there terrified, Mom! What if she is right?" She just sat mirroring me, holding her hands up shrugging her shoulders, saying to me, "Huh?"

"Then the principal tells us while we are in lockdown that the anti-bullying assembly would be cancelled today! Can you believe that? What an idiot! No, he didn't say, 'Don't worry, kids! False alarm. Hey, kids, no bomb.' Duh! What an idiot! Plus, we couldn't leave to go to the cafeteria! So I couldn't eat my lunch! The teacher just looked at us all, and said, 'Oh, well!'" Emily began crying into her hands again.

I didn't even think about what came next. I went over to her and laid her head on my chest, smoothing her hair with my hand, saying "Shhhhhhhh." Through her angry sobs, she continued.

"Then in fifth period, Mom, our teacher made us watch *Hotel Rwanda*. That movie is horrible! They called those people cockroaches! Mother, those innocent children had nowhere to go! It's a true story! That movie is going to give me nightmares!" she shouted the word *nightmares*, as she got up to get a tissue off her dresser. My heart was literally breaking.

I just kept saying to myself, *My poor baby. Our high school students have to worry about so much!* She stood at her dresser, repeating the word *cockroaches.* Trying to approach her to give her a hug, she pulled away from me and went to the corner of her room to sit at her desk.

"Wait, Mom, it gets better! I walked around like a zombie until I got to my seventh period math class. When I walked in, the whole class was talking about the Boston Marathon Bombing. The kids were saying it was horrible that they didn't shoot that boy who helped with the bombing, that the cops should have just gunned him down in the streets so that all the people of Boston could watch him die!" She paused to take a sip of her water and wiped her face with the back of her hand. She took a deep breath and kept speaking.

"All the stupid boys sitting in front of me were laughing and talking about what they hope happens to the terrorists who did it. *Then* they started saying crap about the Muslims who go to our school—how all Muslims are terrorists. I just couldn't take it. I snapped!" she said, straightening herself up in front of me. I don't think I blinked the entire time she spoke.

"I asked the teacher if we could talk about something else. The stupid teacher put his hand up, as if to shush me!" She was standing before me, reenacting the events that took place in her classroom.

She went on, "The kid in front of me turned around and said to me, 'Face it, Emily, shit happens.' That idiot, Joel! I stood up and said to him, 'No, Joel! NO! Shit doesn't *just* happen—unless we chew up all the bullshit in this world *AND* swallow it!' Then I shoved him!" She ended her sentence by flopping on her bed. I moved over to the side of her bed.

Enormous, silent tears rolled down my face. I just started shaking my hands out, as if my subconscious was trying to keep all the pain of those incidents away from me. Too late, these were wounds my heart would never let go of.

As an adult, I lay awake for nights, crying, after the Sandy Hook Elementary shooting. That event, actually all the things she named, made me drop to my knees and ask God, "Why?" I knew her day would have sent me right over the edge, too. I heard Emily say my name.

"Mom, why can't anyone understand? We may be young, but, we are smart, educated kids with feelings! It's not the same, like when you grew up. The world has changed! We are not robots! How much, Mom? How much are we supposed to take?" She was looking at me, shaking her head. I took her in my arms.

I just rocked with her as we hugged each other. I kissed the top of her head. Neither one of said anything to each other for a few moments. I just hugged her, humming no particular song. I was just humming.

Then I heard, from behind me, my son Eddie standing in the doorway. He said, "What are you two freaks doing?" I turned to him and said, "What does it look like, son? We are hugging. Emily had a really bad day today at school." I was surprised Emily didn't stop hugging me. I held her more tightly as I turned to him and gave him a look, an eye roll.

"School is for fools. Later, weirdos! I am going to the gym to work out." I heard him slam the front door. We both started giggling.

"What can I say, Emily?" *Is that all I can say to her?* This made us both start really laughing. I know she was feeling our unspoken bond, the bond we have had since the moment the nurses put her in my arms the second after she was born.

"I wish I could have seen Joel's face when you shoved him," I said to her as she broke free from my arms to go over and wipe the mascara under her eyes.

"Yeah, stupid coward. He put his math book up in front of his face!" She started laughing, bobbing and ducking, holding an invisible book in front of her, reenacting Joel's reaction. I reached out to take her hands in mine. I made eye contact with her.

"I have to be honest, Emily. (I paused, thinking about my next sentence very carefully.) That is the coolest detention I think I have heard of in my entire life. What a difference you are going to make in this world, Em! How? How on earth did I create such an awesome daughter?" I was tapping my hand on my heart as she stood looking at me with her mouth hanging open, twirling a piece of her hair in her fingers.

"I never, ever expected that. I thought you would take my iPhone away or something!" she said, standing directly in front of me grinning. I reached out and wiped a smudge of mascara she missed.

"Nope. Just promise me, though, no more shoving. Deal?" I said, smiling and winking at her.

"Deal! Thank you, Mom," she said to me as she hugged me again, giggling.

"Hey, let's go get some dinner. I am starving, and I know you are hungry. How about breakfast for dinner? Come on; lets go to Denny's." I held up her purse for her to take.

I sat in the restaurant, listening as she read the menu to me, even tough I knew what I was getting. But, it felt good to hear her reading to me. So, I let her read all eight or so pages of the menu. I was thinking to myself, *Good Lord! Denny's has an enormous menu!*

I was also lost in thought, thinking about her day at school. What exactly was I going to do about it? I knew one thing; I resolved to keep a close, close eye on that school from now on. But more importantly, I was going to watch her like a hawk, from a very close distance. I also decided I would wait to tell her about my news

When the waitress came over to take our order, I had Emily go first. When it was my turn, I folded up my menu, looked up to the waitress, and said, "I will have one scrambled egg, one sunny-side-up egg, one over-easy egg, one poached egg, and one omelet. Please. Oh! What kind of toast do you have?" I just sat there, grinning at the waitress. The waitress looked at me like I came in on the four o'clock crazy bus. I blurted out at her, "You know what? Just bring me rye toast. Thank you."

"Mother, seriously? You can't eat all those eggs!" Emily said to me as she pinched her nose, making pretend gagging noises.

"I am only taking a few bites of each egg, Em. I am doing an experiment," I said in a hushed tone over the table to her, handing the menus up to the waitress. She made a face and shrugged her shoulders.

When our check came, Emily's phone started ringing. She gave me the puppy dog eyes, which for some reason made me melt. "Go, go answer your phone. But stand right outside the door. Don't be a rude cell phoner!" She smiled, leaving the booth.

I reached in my purse to get my check card when I saw a little blue envelope. It was the card Sam's wife had brought to me. I had forgotten all about it! My hands trembled as I took it out of my purse. I sat it on the table in front of me for a moment, looking at my name written in beautiful cursive writing. I found myself pleading in my mind, *Swallow the enormous lump in your throat, and do not throw up all those eggs.*

Dear Christine,

My body was tired, my sweet girl. I am sorry I could not give you one last hug. But, it is better this way. I want to remember your smile cheering me on.

Please remember, my sweet girl, you are not here just to fill a space. Nothing would be the same if you did not exist. Every place you have ever been and everyone you have ever spoken to would be different without *you.*

We are all connected; we are all better because of your beautiful spirit.

My dear Christine, I did find my somewhere over the rainbow. It was meeting you on that rainy day, when I walked through your door.

Stay strong, my bluebird. Until we meet again…

—*Sam*

HERE COMES THE SUN— FOR YOU AND ME 17

Well, my dear reader, this is the end. This book is my homage to you. I fell in love with you the moment I put my pen to paper. I am sad–or is it melancholy that I am feeling? I am not sure. I do know that I cried thinking about saying good-bye to you. Then I realized this isn't the end; it is our beginning.

You have become part of my everyday. You kept me motivated, smiling, and inspired! Wherever I was, I was thinking of what I wanted to write to *you*. I was often writing on a scrap piece of paper or waking up in the middle of the night, flipping on my light to find my journal to write down a thought, a poem, a feeling, or a song. I even wrote on my hand! You were never far from me.

I hope this book has filled you with many smiles–and a few tears. I hope you have been saying to yourself, *If she can do it, I surely can!* My mission for you, my plea to you, is to take that first step up your own mountain. It's time, dear reader! Maybe you will even make your own vision board. Trust me. There is nothing in this world that can compare to experiencing new inspiration. The wonder and excitement of awakening the power of your vision will give you hope and promise.

I know! You can write to me; that would make my day! Tell me about your life in the climb. Just promise me, though; if you do write, unplug from technology. I promise writing by hand will engage your heart and allow your spirit to let go of things a little more easily.

Let me explain what a surprise this book gave me. It's like when your great aunt shows up at your birthday party, with a gift wrapped in Christmas paper. You reluctantly take the gift and give a weak smile. You know there are probably two potholders with embroidered cartoon vegetables in the box.

But, NO! You open it, and it's the gift you've only dreamed about owning. It's the gift you have been saving all your pennies for, the gift that you didn't think would ever be yours.

Happy dance! *Christine's Kilimanjaro* has been the greatest gift to me. You, my dear reader, helped me climb to the top of my bright and shiny mountain. The flag now planted at the top of the summit says *YOU* on one side and *ME* on the other. I have been peeling back the layers. I have shared things with you that I have never even spoken to my own mother about. If anyone gave me the courage to peel the layers back, it was *YOU*. I learned, with your help, to keep my eyes open and to stop and enjoy the view along my climb. I have found new courage; many things on my own vision board have come true–like writing this book and meeting someone in 2013 that changed my life for the better forever. So, I am still working on my skinny jeans and meeting Ellen, but I am not going to give up on my vision. Why? Because I believe! I believe that if you write it down, you can make it happen!

I know that I made it to the top, and now I have to climb back down. But, I am not filled with anxiety or fear. I have you and a fresh journal waiting for more words, more stories, more goals, and more promise. I am sure that on my way back down there will be a million more things I didn't face on my way up. But, that's okay. I now challenge whatever comes my way with *you* by my side.

You helped me realize that I am tired of the *status quo* I created for myself! I don't want to stick my toe in the deep end of the pool anymore to check the water's temperature. I want to jump in and do a cannon ball!

And, guess what? Come Saturday morning, the moms at the YMCA are going to be shocked when they see the biggest splash of their lives!

When they look at me, pointing in disgust, I will just float across the pool doing the backstroke. I will think to myself, *Keep looking, ladies. You are just jealous!* I know they haven't lived until they have had someone as special as you in their lives: you, my reader.

Before I share some very exciting news, I need to pay forward a special thank you to two people who are my North Stars. They point the way, tell me to keep going, and always light up my dreams with words of encouragement. They are together in beautiful harmony, my personal cheering section. On bended knee, with arms open wide, I am weeping with gratitude. I weep because of the loving encouragement you gave me when this book was just a figment of my imagination. Jay and Jeannie Levinson, my love for you will transcend through time. Always.

Now, for the good news. Are you sitting down? My lump was not cancer. The day I found out, my doctor called me and gave me the news over the phone. The second I hung up the phone, it started raining. I mean, it was raining farm animals! It was raining too hard to even be considered raining only cats and dogs.

I looked out my kitchen window and thought, *Huh?* Finding my shoes, I thought I would stand out on my front porch and watch the downpour. I put my hand on the front door handle, turned the doorknob, and gently opened the door. With God as my witness, it stopped raining!

Slowly the clouds moved from my front yard, and the sun started peeking through the enormous oak trees. I shook my head and rubbed my eyes like I was in Oz! I swear that I have never seen anything like it!

The only song that came to my mind that moment as I twirled on my sidewalk, looking in all directions of the sky, was a song I knew instantly I would dedicate to *you*. It's "Here Comes the Sun" by The Beatles. Come on, reader. Put your arms up and celebrate with me! You know you love this song!

Little side note: it's two sugars and light cream (for my coffee), and my favorite color is rainbow. Nothing in my house matches any more, and I LOVE it! I painted my front door red, which freaked my daughter out. Why? Because she said our house is now painted in Ohio State colors. I do like two-ply toilet paper after all, and I happen to hate eggs! After I was done sampling them that night at Denny's, I went home and had a bowl of Cheerios. I never say the word *fine* anymore. Instead, I say *fabulous*. I also made a change jar for our house in Africa for special needs children. I go to church by myself if no one wants to go with me, and I visit the ocean at least once a month. Dear reader, it is the small stuff. XOXO

Playlist for my reader:

You didn't really think I could say good-bye to you that easily, did you? (LOL)

1. "What Makes You Beautiful"–One Direction
   (I'm still not giving up the dream of dancing with Emily, One Direction, and Ellen!)
2. "With or Without You"–U2
   (The song playing on my ride down in the elevator with my co-workers.)
3. "Low Rider"–War
   (The song Emily and I danced to in the kitchen, when we talked about being on *Ellen.*)
4. "Dancing Queen"–ABBA
   (The song I wanted to listen to before I got in the car accident.)
5. "Personal Jesus"–Depeche Mode
   (The song playing when I met Ed in the nightclub.)
6. "Teenage Mutant Ninja Turtles Theme Song"
   (A song that played at my house for six months straight when my son was four.)
7. "Hotel California"–The Eagles
   (The song playing when Javi picked me up for our first date.)
8. "We Belong"–Pat Benatar
   (The song that Daren played the entire way home from New Jersey.)
9. "Walking on Broken Glass"–Annie Lennox
   (The song I sang during my shower concert.)

10. "You're So Vain"–Carly Simon

    (The song I sang during my closet concert.)

11. "Blister in the Sun"–Violent Femmes

    (The song I talked about on our boat ride to Put-In-Bay.)

12. "Let the River Run"–Carly Simon

    (The song the choir sang during my moving gospel experience.)

13. "Lighters"–Eminem, featuring Bruno Mars

    (This song that was my writing music for the New Jersey chapter.)

14. "Rocket Man"–Elton John

    (The song I always sing to Ed before he leaves because it makes him laugh.)

15. "Every Little Thing She Does Is Magic"–The Police

    (The song Ed sent me after I called him in parking lot.)

16. "Fire and Rain"–James Taylor

    The song I sang lying on bathroom floor, thinking about life.

17. "Here Comes the Sun"–The Beatles

    (The song I dedicate to you.)

18. "Anything Could Happen"–Ellie Goulding

    (The song I played when I finished the book, and everyone danced with me.)

Stay strong, my dear reader–until we meet again.

Just in case you want to write about your own magical climb, email me: kilimanjarocm@yahoo.com